HOME CARE HOW TO

The Guide To Starting Your Senior In Home Care Business

BRENDAN JOHN

ACACIA Publishing

COPYRIGHT

Published by ACACIA Publishing
Division of The ACACIA Group, LLC.
Visit us at www.TheAcaciaGroupLLC.com

United States of America.

Cover Art: Albert C. Francisco.

ACACIA Publishing publishes its books in a variety of print and electronic formats. Some content that appears in print may not be available in electronic books and vice versa. For more information about ACACIA Publishing products, visit our web site at www.theacaciagroupllc.com. For general information on our other products and services or for technical support, please contact us at acaciapublishing@theacaciagroupllc.com.

Library of Congress Cataloging-in-Publication Data:

John, Brendan

HOME CARE HOW TO - The Guide To Starting Your Senior In Home Care Business
Brendan John. 1st Edition
p. cm.
Includes Bibliographical references and index (p.).

1. Business – Success. 2. Small Business – Management. 3. Entrepreneurship.

ISBN 13 - 978-098-318-320-4
ISBN 10 -   098-318-320-1

Printed in the United States of America.
10 9 8 7 6 5 4 3 2 1

ACKNOWLEDGEMENTS

Many people helped transform this book from an idea into a reality. Some may not be aware of how their help made a difference.

Several require special mention. Thank you to my family for the encouragement, support and love. I'm blessed with an awesome family and thank God each day for every member. Laura, your late hours and hard work editing makes the book flow and not ramble. Al, Peter, and Joe, your ongoing vision, guidance, inspiration and mentorship is priceless. Thank you! To the team who helped make the production of this book possible - thank you!

I also thank *you*, the reader. Without you and your desire to help our cherished elders and succeed in starting your own senior care business, this book wouldn't have been written. My hope and intention for you is tremendous success, happiness and joy in your service to the many seniors we are truly blessed to learn and grow from. May this book be just the beginning of your successful service to others!

"The starting point of all achievement is desire"
~ Napoleon Hill ~

LIMITS OF LIABILITY

While the publisher, designers, contributors, editors, and author have used their best efforts in preparing Home Care How To, they make no warranties or representations with respect to the accuracy or completeness of the contents of this book and specifically disclaim any implied warranties or merchantability or finances for a particular purpose. It is further acknowledged that no warranty, of any kind, may be created or extended by any written sales materials or sales representatives.

The advice and strategies contained herein may not be suitable for your situation and do contain risk, including the risk of financial loss. Always consult with a financial or legal professional when and where appropriate before undertaking any action. Users of this material assume all risk. Neither the publisher, designers, editors, contributors, nor author shall be liable for any loss of profit or any other commercial damages, including but not limited to financial, special, incidental, consequential, or other damages.

TABLE OF CONTENTS

Chapter 7
PREPARE FINANCIAL SYSTEMS

Chapter 8
HIRING CARE PROVIDERS

PREFACE

The Baby Boomer population includes those born between 1946 and 1964. The first of this generation is reaching their golden years. Over the next 25 years, the number of individuals age 65+ years in the United States will blossom from 35 million to over 70 million, and the demand for products and services that provide their care will grow at rates never seen before.

This growing demand for home care puts you in the right place at the right time. The opportunities are enormous! Entering the senior care service industry is exciting and rewarding and gives you the ability to affect positive change in the lives of seniors and their families while generating a significant income for yourself.

Given that you're considering starting a business of serving seniors, you're probably aware of these growing needs. But it takes more than understanding basic demographics to successfully serve seniors. You need to be a caring, compassionate, empathetic, loving, and understanding person.

Yet the traits alone won't make you successful, either. To successfully grow a profitable in-home senior care business, you'll need to combine the character qualities with specific knowledge, systems, and skills. This book will provide you with the knowledge you need to plan, set up, and implement systems needed to start and operate the successful senior home care company you desire.

This is not a get rich quick manual. Any entrepreneurial venture requires hard work, lots of effort, dedication, and commitment. Serving seniors can be quite challenging and demanding at times, and the personal growth and financial rewards you'll gain through improving others lives can be tremendously rewarding.

Home Care How To is based on the model of creating systems for your business outlined in *The E Myth by Michael Gerber*. If you haven't read that book already, get it today and read it now. Doing so will help you understand the basis of this book's instruction, the importance of systems from the start, and most importantly how you perceive and operate your business.

The book makes many suggestions and recommendations; however, this is not a legal manual, and it's recommended that you consult an attorney about legal questions and a CPA and tax attorney for financial related matters. It's also recommended that you stay plugged in to groups of other in home care business owners.

"If you can dream it, then you can achieve it! You will get all you want in life if you help enough other people get what they want."
~ Zig Ziglar ~

INTRODUCTION

Congratulations! You've decided to improve your own life by creating your own business helping the rapidly growing number of seniors—enriching, enhancing, and prolonging their lives by helping them stay where they want to stay: in their own homes. With today's Baby Boomers beginning to reaching their golden years, you're in the right place at the right time.

This material is a culmination of over 10 years of experience, research, consulting, and service to thousands of seniors through the founding and developing of numerous successful senior care companies and networking with and providing consulting guidance to other senior care business owners around the nation.

Home Care How To was created to help you plan, prepare for, and apply the actions necessary to start and operate your company. It will walk you step by step through what you need to do to set up your business, launch it, and prepare for growth.

Close your eyes and imagine what your business will look like in one year, three years, and five years. Picture who you will become as a successful business owner already having achieved your dream, helping hundreds or thousands of seniors stay in their own home. Does this excite you? I thought so. This book is intended to help you achieve that success you dream of.

To further help in getting your start-up operational, *HOME CARE How To* has an accompanying website where you can access downloadable forms and documents shown throughout the book as well as further assistance to help with your business venture.

Setting up your own agency is not rocket science. This book will cover what you need to do to get yours going. To include every morsel of information you'll want to get your particular business going would take far more than the few hundred pages included here. However, you can move forward confidently knowing that if you need additional help specific to your venture, business set-up classes, one-on-one coaching and other resources are readily available at *www.homecarehowto.com.* Be sure to take advantage of the introductory business coaching offers available to anyone who has purchased this book.

This book periodically refers to and suggests helpful website addresses. Whether you choose to use the websites, their products and services offered is up to you. They are simply recommendations to assist you in your venture. As you conduct your research and choose vendors and tools to help build your business, make sure to check references and do your due diligence. Feel free to use other services that you have discovered and may work best for you. If you find a website, company, product, or service that you find especially helpful, I'd love to hear about it!

At the end of each chapter is a task list guide. Read each chapter in its entirety. You may already know about one topic or another; however, reading each chapter will help you understand the full context of the steps that follow and may also spark other ideas you've not thought of—and single-handedly give you a whole new perspective to your business.

Chapter 1 starts with a key question everyone must ask before they even start: Is starting a home care business is right for you?
Many people aspire to own their own business; however, it takes more than just a dream to make a business succeed. We'll discuss the traits, skills, and mindset necessary to start and operate your own business and look at some of the most common reasons businesses fail.

Chapter 2 helps you understand the business of senior care. We'll discuss your clientele—seniors—so you have a good understanding of who they are, their needs, and their fears.

You'll also learn about the different types of home care agencies and what kinds of services you'll probably provide and how they benefit your clients and their families. We'll discuss differences between independent agencies and franchises, operations, and staffing overviews.

Chapter 3 is about research—researching and analyzing the market/area you plan to serve, your competition, and the state laws and licensing requirements for your market.

Chapter 4 is about actually setting up your business, creating action, and seeing results quickly. You'll be creating your company name, logo, and business entity and taking the actions required so your company complies with laws and licensing requirements. You'll also be setting up your office with the tools necessary to prepare for success.

Chapter 5 discusses the essential topic of creating the blueprint for your company: a business plan. Without it, you'll be setting yourself up for failure.

Chapter 6 will teach you about the systems to put into place to operate your home care services. We'll discuss your contacts management program and scheduling systems. You'll also learn to create your introductory commercials and scripts so you know what to say when people ask you what you're doing.

Chapter 7 teaches you about the financial systems you'll need to create. You'll learn about accounting software, the necessity of hiring a financial expert, setting up your payroll, and the importance of insurance coverage. We'll also discuss employee rates and set up the service rates.

Chapter 8 covers hiring the staff to perform the services you offer. We'll look at who your ideal care provider is and how to go find the very best. You'll be setting up systems for seeking, attracting, interviewing, and hiring new employees as well as their ongoing training and overall management .

Chapter 9 discusses the process of obtaining your business' lifeblood: new clients. We'll cover what your ideal clients look like and how to obtain them. Once you have them, managing relationships with them becomes key in sustaining them.

Chapter 10 lays out the steps for marketing your services to garner more clients. You'll learn where to market your services and how to get leads. Then we'll talk about what to do with the leads as your marketing systems begin working.

Assuming you go through each of the chapters and complete each step, by the end of the book you should have your business up and running and your phone should be ringing very soon, if not already. So let's get busy, one step at a time.

Onward to Chapter One!

CHAPTER 1

IS A HOME CARE BUSINESS RIGHT FOR YOU?

So you want to start your own senior home care business. You're not alone. In this world of constant technological advancements, increased corporate downsizing, international use of the internet, and growing demand for personalized products and services, starting a business has become easier than ever before.

But while it's easier than ever to get a business started, it's also easier to fail. So, before you plunge in and just start a company, you need to ask some essential questions and complete steps to determine if this will work for you. After all, you're considering a venture that will require investments from almost every aspect of your life—financial, emotional, personal, and physical—not to mention a tremendous amount of time.

In this first chapter, you'll learn about the crucial questions you should ask yourself before you jump in. You'll learn the critical first steps to take to form and prepare your business.

Self Analysis: Do You Have What It Takes?

To Start Any Business

By now you've probably considered this question. At first, it sounds very simple: You set your own hours, no one tells you how to do your job, you make the decisions, and a boss won't lay you off. You're in control! Well, sort of. Starting your own business is an adventure that comes with no guarantees. Many risks are involved with launching any business. But with the proper foresight, plans, and preparation you can reduce those risks and improve your chances for success.

Begin by looking inside yourself to evaluate your strengths and weaknesses. Ask yourself these important questions about becoming an entrepreneur:

Do you have the physical energy and emotional stamina to run a business?

Starting and owning a business is a lot of work. It's been said that when you own your own business you can work half-days all the time. And that is true—you get to pick which 12 hours each day to work, six and seven days per week.

Are you a good decision maker?

Remember when you dreamed of not having a boss telling you what to do? The flip side there is no one to tell you what decision to make. You must be able to make quick decisions, often under pressure, that affect your business both short term and long term.

Are you a go-getter and self-disciplined?

How well do you manage your time? It's up to you to make things happen. You will need to organize and prioritize your time to create projects, schedule appointments, follow up, delegate tasks, and manage the details of each.

Are you a people person?

How well do you deal with people? In business, especially senior care and other services, people skills are a must. You'll be establishing essential relationships with banks, lawyers, employees, vendors, accountants, and, most importantly, clients. Can you deal with unhappy clients, unruly employees, and pushy vendors?

Are you organized?

The ability to plan and organize will save you tremendous amounts of time, headaches, and money as your business grows. Organized systems for schedules, finances, staff, and inventory (to name a few) are essential to smooth operations.

Are you motivated?

After you've put in months of 12 to 16 hour days and the excitement wears off, can you maintain the motivation necessary to follow through on your plans? Burnout is a major contributor to business failure; self-motivation will be a strong factor in surviving burnout and slow times.

Do you and your family understand how your family will be affected?

Support and understanding from your family will be essential as you launch your business and make it profitable. Your business will require much of your time. You may experience financial hardships for months or even years.

To Enter the Home Care Industry

Succeeding in the Senior Home Care business requires a particular set of qualities and capabilities. If you don't possess every single one of the qualities, that's okay, because in many cases you can hire individuals who do have the qualities you lack.

These traits will be very helpful as you begin your venture:

1) Basic compassion, understanding, empathy and desire to serve elderly patients with illnesses.
2) Ability to build a network of individuals and institutions related to the care industry.
3) Solid understanding of the basic business financial aspects of a service.
4) Being a people person who is able to manage a growing staff.

Why Businesses Fail

The passion, energy, and excitement that business ownership can bring do not automatically translate to business success. Starting your own business is risky, with no guarantees, so arm yourself with facts before you begin. Statistically, your chances of success are against you. According to the Small Business Administration, approximately 65 percent of small businesses succeed for the first two years; however, only 44 percent will last four years.

The biggest causes of business failure can be debated. Regardless, there are plenty of catalysts that, if considered during planning and execution, can improve your chances of success by helping you avoid the fatal mistakes:

Undercapitalization:

In each of these areas, the key words are be realistic.

Startup Funds

Don't spend your seed money too quickly. Instead

- Map out a realistic plan for profitability.

- Add in reserve funds.

- Ensure that you have enough seed capital to cover the period of time it takes to reach profitability.

- Manage your finances diligently. Grow only as your revenue allows you to grow, not as your big ideas hope it will grow.

Too Much Overhead

Don't "bite off more than you can chew." Instead, let your revenue dictate your overhead and hiring practices. Before you add to your overhead expenses, increase your revenues. Basing your initial overhead on aggressive projections will soon deplete your capital.

Borrowed Funds

Many businesses borrow too much money, mismanage the funds, and then don't have enough income to repay the loans. These businesses fail.

Personal Use of Business Funds

Don't mingle personal funds with your business. The IRS hates it, and it leads to messy accounting practice and, ultimately, business failure.

Overinvesting in Fixed Assets

Start small. This means, for example, renting a small place that's affordable instead of buying the big building you got a great deal on to grow into.

Location, Location, Bad Location

Because a home care business doesn't require a retail storefront business, the location issue relates more to location within a city or cities that have a large and growing population of citizens age 65 and older for you to serve. A home care office doesn't have to be in a high-rent area. It's more important that you're easily accessible within the area you will serve. If your office is inconvenient for staff or potential clients, you will lose good staff and clients. A strategically placed office/business location can drive traffic to you and increase visibility.

Poor or No Business Plan

You wouldn't build a house without blueprints, would you? But many who start businesses fail to consider the importance of a plan. Creating a business plan requires that you think about the future of your business, the challenges you'll face, and how you'll accomplish your goals. You'll need to think through your competition, financial needs, organizational structure, marketing strategy, and employment management plans. You can accomplish this with the Business Plan Template provided in this system.

No Change

If there is one thing certain in business, it is change. To survive, you must recognize opportunities and adapt your business accordingly.

Ineffective Marketing

Many businesses fail because their owners think customers should find them. You should always be seeking the customers in addition to helping them to find you! Learn cost-effective advertising, and meet lots of people. (Advertising will be discussed in further chapters.)

Not Knowing Your Competition

If you don't do what's necessary to take care of your customers, your competition will.

The above list isn't all-inclusive, of course. Businesses fail for other reasons as well. But this list is a solid start to considering whether starting your own business is right for you. These caveats are provided not to frighten you but rather to prepare you for what lies ahead. Underestimating what it takes to start any business is by far one of the largest—yet surmountable—obstacles that entrepreneurs face. Success can be yours if you're willing to work hard, act on all the steps, and persevere through challenging times.

If you have answered these questions and decided that starting a home care business is still right for you, then it's time to get started.

Chapter 1 Review Task List

After each chapter you'll find a Chapter Review Task List. As you complete each chapter, review the task list; check off each task you've already completed, and address the remaining activities.

Some tasks have contingencies and require time to complete. Move on to another task until the contingencies are met, and then return to finish the task. Make sure you go back and review the task lists periodically to ensure that you've completed each task from each chapter.

Upon completing Chapter 1 you should have:

- ☐ A thorough self analysis.

- ☐ A clear objective of what you're looking for in a business for yourself.

- ☐ Confidence in yourself (and your partner, if applicable) that you have what it takes to succeed in the home care business.

- ☐ A good understanding of why businesses fail.

- ☐ A commitment to not repeat the common mistakes made that lead to business failure.

- ☐ Decided that starting a home care business is right for you.

If you haven't accomplished each task, ask yourself why. Do you need more information before making a decision? Research each area more in depth to help you with your decisions. Is the problem procrastination? Ask why you're procrastinating. Take the time to understand the root reason, because if you're procrastinating small steps in setting up a business, what will you procrastinate while you're in business?

CHAPTER 2

UNDERSTANDING THE BUSINESS OF SENIOR HOME CARE

The senior care industry is in the service business of providing non-medical companion care for seniors in their own homes, allowing them to remain where they often prefer to be. Senior home care is one of the fastest growing industries in the United States, largely because of increased life expectancy and the demographics of the baby boom population. Working children of senior citizens are seeking high quality, honest home care companies that can tend to their aging parents' needs. In fact, according to Careerbuilder.com the home care industry alone will add a projected 1.5 million care provider jobs between 2010 - 2018.

The services that your senior home care business will offer are clearly in growing demand. The rewards you'll receive are numerous: You'll be helping those who want, need, and appreciate your services. You'll also be contributing to economic growth of the nation by offering gainful employment to others while gaining financial rewards that reflect all the good you're doing for people in your community.

You'll need to understand as much as possible about this business. While this book offers a great overview of the industry, you must also continue educating yourself, beyond this book, in all the areas that affect seniors.

All About Today's Seniors

Senior lifestyles, activities, and individual abilities vary greatly due to lifestyles, genetics, individual life experiences, and beliefs. The safe generalization about seniors is that they are like everyone else—individuals. Age alone doesn't dictate one's mental or physical state. Some 85-year-olds are more youthful in appearance and lifestyle than some 65-year-olds. Some seniors are active and social, while others are quiet and reserved. The greater your belief and effort in understanding each individual client will help you immeasurably in showing them the benefits of your providing the very best personalized care possible.

Individual diversity aside, we can still draw some conclusions about seniors:

❖ Seniors, when given the choice, prefer to stay in their own home.

❖ Seniors are historians with long memories and are eager to share these memories with those they love and those who love to learn.

❖ Seniors are surprisingly happy. They mourn their losses and read obituaries; still, the older they get, the more they make peace with who they are and what they've accomplished.

❖ Many seniors are not able to move with ease. Some depend on walkers or wheelchairs. Some don't. In general, though, seniors find it more difficult to climb stairs and take long walks

❖ Seniors have helped shape the community into what it is today. They've articulated the vision of what it should be and developed the programs that serve its members.

❖ Seniors could often use a volunteer to help with ordinary household tasks that are now beyond their ability. For example, they may fear falling when they walk the dog or lack the hand dexterity needed to wash dishes or do laundry.

❖ Seniors' hearing and sight is often not as keen as it once was. Speaking clearly and more slowly to seniors can help them be attentive and engaged in conversation.

❖ Aging adults often prefer to stay active and do so by keeping part-time jobs, volunteering, or having an active social calendar.

❖ Seniors are capable and eager to learn new things. While change may be difficult for them, with enough time and repetition they are able to pick up new skills and knowledge while keeping their minds and bodies active.

❖ Response time usually diminishes as people age. This affects driving, conversations, and daily living activities.

❖ Seniors love to invest in the future by connecting with younger generations. They need solid relationships with adults (family and others) who have an interest in a particular skill or career.

❖ Seniors need to feel useful. Many have cared for others their whole lives and find it difficult to always now be the one receiving help. They might not be able to do as much as they could when they were younger, but they have much to offer others.

Common Health Ailments of Seniors

❖ Dementia—including Alzheimer's disease.

❖ Depression.

❖ Heart conditions (i.e., congestive heart failure, high blood pressure, hypertension, coronary artery disease, and vascular disease).

❖ Incontinence.

❖ Arthritis.

❖ Diminished sense of smell or taste, which can lead to dehydration and smaller appetites.

- ❖ Osteoporosis, which weakens the bones. A simple fall can cause much more damage than it would have before.

- ❖ Diabetes.

- ❖ Parkinson's disease.

- ❖ Diminished eyesight (glaucoma, macular degeneration).

- ❖ Cancer.

- ❖ Thinner skin—wounds don't heal as quickly.

- ❖ Weakened immune systems, which lengthen recovery times and diminish the body's ability to resist diseases or bacteria.

- ❖ Suicide is a growing concern with the elderly By age 85, suicide rates for the elderly jump significantly; causes include loneliness and physical problems.

Greatest Fears of Seniors

Although many seniors prefer to stay active, various fears may prevent them from doing that. In national surveys, the following come up continually as senior's greatest fears:

- ❖ Declining health.

- ❖ Loss of independence.

- ❖ Being compelled to do things against their will.

- ❖ Falling or hurting themselves.

- ❖ No longer being able to drive.

- ❖ Loss of personal autonomy,

- ❖ Inability to manage their own daily living activities.

- ❖ Being placed in a nursing home.

❖ Running out of money.

❖ Alzheimer's disease.

Demographics, Trends and Stats of Baby Boomers

America's Baby Boomers (those born between 1946 and 1964) are setting new records with the numbers of people over 65 years old.

❖ In 2001, there were 35 million Americans over the age of 65.

❖ In 2011, 10,000 people will be turning 65 each year. Eighty-five percent will at some point require some sort of in-home care assistance.

❖ By 2025, 62 million Americans will be age 65 or older. That's almost double in 25 years. The fastest growing segment of our population is the 85 and older group, and half of them need some help with personal care.

❖ By 2030, 70 million Americans will be over 65. This is one out of every five Americans.

❖ In 2006, Baby Boomers age 42 to 60 totaled an estimated 78.0 million and made up 26.1 percent of the total U.S. population.

❖ In 2011, Baby Boomers are now between 47 and 65 years old, which lends itself to say that there is growth for the next 25+ years!

As the elder boom population grows, the number of those living with health problems and need care grows:

❖ About 80 percent of seniors have at least one chronic health condition, and 50 percent have at least two. Arthritis, hypertension, heart disease, diabetes, and respiratory disorders are some of the leading causes of activity limitations among older people

* Thirty percent of family care providers caring for seniors are themselves 65 or over; another 15 percent are between the ages of 45 to 54.

* After age 65, an American has more than a 70 percent chance of needing help with the activities of daily living such as dressing, bathing, and using the bathroom.

* 8.9 million care providers (20 percent of adult care providers) care for someone 50 years or older who has dementia.

* Forty-eight percent of care providers reported using at least one of seven outside services (e.g., transportation, home-delivered meals, respite, etc.) to supplement their caregiving.

And that's just the beginning! According to Third Age, a Boomer's Guide to a Life of Health, Happiness, Passion, and Purpose:

* The average life expectancy at the turn of 1900 was 47. 2010 projections are 75.6 for males and 81.4 for females.

* An estimated 43 percent of Americans age 65 or older will spend time in a nursing home.

* By 2012, 75 percent of Americans over age 65 will require long-term care. Long-term care costs are rising at 6 percent annually.

* 59 percent of the adult population either is or expects to be a family care provider, and 2 million more care providers will be needed in the next 20 years.

* Alzheimer's disease does not happen overnight. It begins to affect the brain 10 to 20 years before the first symptoms appear.

* Increasing age is the greatest risk factor for Alzheimer's. One in 10 individuals over 65, and nearly half over 85 are affected. Rare, inherited forms of

Alzheimer's can strike individuals in their 30s and 40s.

❖ A person with Alzheimer's disease will live an average of eight years but as many as 20 years or more from the first onset of symptoms.

❖ More than 7 out of 10 people with Alzheimer's disease live at home, where family and friends provide 75 percent of their care.

❖ Half of all nursing home residents have Alzheimer's disease or a related disorder. The average cost for nursing home care is $42,000 per year but can exceed $70,000 The average length of stay in a nursing home is 2.5 years.

❖ The annual cost of Alzheimer's care in the U.S. is at least $100 billion, and it will soar to at least $375 billion by mid-century, overwhelming our health care system and bankrupting Medicare and Medicaid.

❖ Medicare costs for beneficiaries with Alzheimer's are expected to increase 75 percent, from $91 billion in 2005 to $160 billion in 2010. Medicaid expenditures on residential dementia care will increase 14 percent, from $21 billion to $24 billion.

❖ Medicare expenditures for people with Alzheimer's are nearly three times higher than the average for all beneficiaries. Half of all Medicare beneficiaries with dementia also receive Medicaid, because they have exhausted their own resources for their care.

❖ Older middle-aged Americans who report disabilities related to mobility increased significantly from 1997 to 2007.

Read more at Third Age (www.thirdage.com) – A Boomers Guide

Clientele

The ideal clientele for non-medical senior home care services are elder adults ages 65 to 100+ who are generally ambulatory or semi-ambulatory, able to function and remain living in their own home, and simply require some assistance with activities of daily living such as laundry, meal preparation, light housekeeping, and transportation. They may have varying stages of memory loss such as or Alzheimer's disease or other diagnoses such as Parkinson's or Lou Gehrig's disease (ALS). Your ideal client wants to stay at home and is able to provided he or she receives help with some activities of daily living. We'll discuss in more detail your ideal-client profile in Chapter 9.

Types of Home Care

There are two primary types of care in the home care industry: medical home care, often referred to as home health, and non-medical home care, known as supportive care. This book provides focus on the non-medical side, though the framework of the business isn't much different from home health.

Home Health Care Services are prescribed by doctor's specific orders and carried out by licensed nurses, nurse practitioners, and nurse assistants. These medical services include wound care, vital sign check-ups, and medication administration. Often these services are covered by insurance programs such as Medicare or Medicaid. Home health licensure requirements are carefully regulated by federal and state laws, which can vary by state. Home health businesses typically require more involved licensure process to qualify and must be approved for operation

Non-medical care services have less demanding licensure requirements than home health agencies do. In many states these requirements are minimal; states with stricter requirements include Florida and New York. Non-medical (supportive care) services, typically performed by experienced care providers, home health aides (HHA), and certified nurse's assistant (CNA), include assistance with meal preparation and clean-up, light housekeeping, laundry, transportation to appointments and other events, medication reminders, bathing, dressing, and grooming.

Services You'll Provide

Essentially, you'll be providing first-rate care and services to seniors who need some assistance to remain in their own home by hiring and training exceptional care providers and matching them with seniors who need this assistance. People with developmental and mental disabilities also need these services. For the sake of continuity, this book focuses on senior care.

The core services non-medical agencies provide consist of:

Meal Preparation

Most seniors have certain dietary restrictions that require regularly scheduled, healthy meals. Taste buds and palates weaken as people age; to compensate for diminished tastes seniors often consume a larger amount of salty or sweet foods.

Laundry

Seniors' energy levels diminish from their younger years. Vision impairment is also an issue. The simple task of laundry can wipe the energy from a senior.

Light Housekeeping

Impaired vision and lower energy levels often make light housekeeping a low priority. The light housekeeping services you'll offer are intended to keep the home tidy, not provide a deep cleaning of the home. Care providers can help coordinate and oversee the supervision of a professional home cleaning service for more thorough house cleaning.

Companionship

Working children aren't able to visit as often—or at all—so seniors can become isolated at home if support systems aren't put in place. Depression can isolate them even more. Care providers can help bring the seniors into the community by accompanying them to a movie, taking them to visit other friends, driving them to church, going to the library, and accompanying them to other activities.

Shopping, Errands, and Incidental Transportation

Care providers assist seniors by running errands such as going to the post office or grocery store. Because many seniors have diminishing eyesight and are no longer (or should no longer be) driving, care providers assist by providing the necessary transportation for their activities—e.g., doctor appointments, hair appointments, picking up medications, or escorting them to church or other social activities.

Medication Reminders

Forgetting to take medications, taking the wrong medication, or taking extra doses because they forgot if they took it earlier can be harmful. Care providers assist with self-administered medications by reminding seniors it's time to take them.
NOTE: Care providers do not administer or touch the medication.

Bathing, Dressing, and Grooming

One of the greatest risk of falls occurs in the shower; seniors may bathe less often than before because they fear falling, have less energy, have impaired memory, or simply don't care anymore. Buttons and zippers are difficult to fasten; diminished use of hands and fingers makes dressing more difficult. A compassionate care provider can assist with these tasks while boosting the senior's self esteem in the process.

Benefits Clients and Families Receive

Everyone loves the comfort and familiarity of their own homes and seniors are as much if not more inclined to stay in their homes as long as they can. Providing in home care services benefits clients and family in many ways including:

❖ Clients maintain their privacy, dignity and independence when they are in control of their care and environment.

❖ Improving relationships and familial support while keeping the family together.

❖ Peace of mind to families that know their loved one(s) are safe.

❖ Maximum independence, comfort and dignity for the client.

❖ Preventing hospital visits or nursing home care.

❖ A more active lifestyle. Individualized care customized to the individual client and family.

❖ Cost savings compared with that of facility or hospital care.

❖ Reduced family stress—the family does not have to worry about the care they have little time to provide.

❖ Increased quality time with family. Children of aging parents are often already strapped of time.

The "Sandwich Generation" find themselves stretched among the responsibilities of raising their own children, working, and caring for their parents. Social visits to the parents may turn into visits to help them with things they can no longer do for themselves. Increased demands can make them late to work (or cause them to leave early) or use up their vacation and personal time. The children may develop feelings of resentfulness — or guilt, if they believe that they are not doing enough for their parents.

Thanks to the services you provide, the children are now able to enjoy social visits with their parents and spend more quality time with them. They experience less stress because they no longer have to worry about the limited time available between work and their own children's activities. They can focus on their work when they're working and focus on their children's activities when they're with the children.

A different situation may include children who have become "empty nesters." They've recently retired and have been looking forward to traveling and spending more time together, focusing on activities they've thought and dreamed about for years. Availing themselves of your care services reduces the stress and resentment by allowing them to continue with their plans while knowing their parents' needs are being met.

Franchise, Independent, Membership or Acquisition?

When you open your home care company you have options. Each involves pros and cons:

❖ Purchase a franchise, which assigns you a specific territory and follows a set system; you agree to follow their guidelines and limitations.

❖ Start and operate an independent home care agency, defining the communities you serve without limits, creating your systems and processes based on what works for your company (this book helps you do that),

❖ Buy into a membership organization that provides training for setup and systems for operations. Ongoing support is provided for monthly fees.

❖ Buy an existing, already operating home care business with existing client base and staff.

With an independent agency, you forge your own path. You create the business model that works best for you with only the limitations that you place for yourself and company. You call the shots. Start-up costs are significantly lower, as there's no upfront franchise or membership fees. You choose which services to provide. Your service area is as large or small as you decide. If you wish to expand your service area, you can do so immediately without permission or added fees. Your bottom line isn't diminished by ongoing monthly royalty fees.

It's also up to you to find and put together the ongoing support of other like-minded business owners. You'll need to develop your own support network of business owners and managers. Ads and logos are up to you to design, change, and experiment with as you see fit. You're also responsible for coming up with new, fresh ideas to stay ahead of your competition.

When the word *franchise* is mentioned people often think of McDonald's, Taco Bell, or other fast food. In reality, franchising has become common in just about every industry, including the many that target seniors and home care.

Franchises provide systems for startup and operations, one to two weeks of training usually at the franchise headquarters and a specific territory to serve in exchange for an upfront investment of $14K to $100K. Once trained, you'll head home to implement the systems they teach you. In addition to the franchise purchase cost, when you start generating revenue, plan to cut an ongoing monthly royalty fee check of 2 to 8 percent of gross revenues. The ongoing royalty fees are in exchange for using the franchise name, ongoing support, and varying levels of shared marketing/advertising expenses. Some franchisors will require that you have an office location (not a home office) from the beginning, which is fine yet adds to upfront cash requirements.

Ongoing support varies among franchisors but can include phone support, newsletters, marketing guidelines, software use or discounts, conference calls with the other franchise members to exchange ideas and compare strategies, and some have annual meetings. Most franchisors limit the territory you can service and contractually lock you in the franchise agreement for 5 to 10 years. If you wish to expand your territory, you'll need to invest additional fees if another franchisee hasn't already claimed that area. If you get a call from a client in an area covered by another franchisee, you usually need to hand the client to that franchisee.

Purchasing a franchise system does not guarantee your success in the industry, any more than choosing the independent agency and going on your own will. The common phrase amongst franchisors is "you're in business for yourself but not by yourself", however keep in mind that franchisors are not in the same business as you. They are in the business of selling franchise territories. Your sales are focused on helping other clients to stay in their own home. If you were to part ways in your relationship with them or you go out of business, you've lost your upfront investment and the ability to go on your own in that area to strike on your own independently for the 5-10 years they've locked you into. However, rarely do their contracts restricted them from selling another franchise in that same area after you've closed doors. Work with a lawyer to review, negotiate and understand the franchise contracts completely.

Beginning an agency by becoming part of a Membership organization is another alternative. A membership usually has a lot of the benefits of a franchise without taking a percentage of your income in royalties. Plan to invest an initial upfront amount of $10K to $30K to get the training, tools and start-up guidance. Often considerably less than franchises, the membership organizations typically charge a flat rate each month instead of a percentage of gross revenues. As your company grows, the monthly rate remains the same. The information and support provided by the organization doesn't change as you grow, so the fixed rate can be attractive over time.

Obtaining a home care agency by acquisition is also an option to enter the industry. Buying an existing business can provide instant cash flow, clientele, staff, office, marketing and sales operations and reputation. There are often home care agencies for sale which have been around for 5 to 10 years and depending on many variables, vary in cost. Being able to buy these resources already functioning can be a tremendous benefit and allow rapid growth. The flip side is that if it's done improperly it can prove more of a burden than you bargained for.

Buying someone else's business is not for the faint of heart. It requires significant amount of market research, due diligence, business saavy, proper timing, great negotiation and more. If you're considering this route, the information covered in this book should be extremely useful as you investigate the basics of how an existing home care agency business needs to operate. Whether you've never owned a business before or have an extensive business background, always consult with your professional team including an attorney, experienced business brokers and accountant.

Whichever route you choose, do your research. If a franchisor provides you demographics and research information, verify this research with your own. Creating the systems isn't difficult. It takes time and thought and once they are in place, you're simply repeating and improving on their processes. The question becomes how much do you want to invest upfront for getting those systems up and running? How much of your profits are you willing to part with for ongoing support each month after those systems are in place and running?

Systems of Business Operation

Operations are key to any business that has long term success: How is the business run?

Within the seemingly simplistic question are numbers of ways to approach how things get done. Some business owners think that if they want something done right, they need to do it themselves. Staff quickly learns they can't do anything right—so they leave or let the business owner do everything. Other owners think that they shouldn't have to do anything. In turn, staff follows the leadership of doing nothing, and nothing ever gets done.

Owners who do everything eventually burn out, give up, or feel stuck. Owners who do nothing find that their businesses fail. Successful business owners and managers usually understand that the happy medium lies within the systems of operations and hiring the right people who do things better than the owner.

Operations succeed when they are designed around systems and the systems are run by people. If systems aren't in place, then the business runs the people—a fast track to chaos, burnout, and turnover. If you haven't already read the book *The E Myth*, get it now and read it. Pay attention to what it says about systems running your business. That concept alone will allow you to build your business from the ground up, putting systems in place so as your company grows, you are able to manage and maintain life balance with family, hobbies, and sanity.

Chapter 2 review Task List

Upon completing Chapter 2 you should:

❑ Understand today's senior lifestyles.

❑ Understand common physical ailments of seniors.

❑ Understand the common fears of seniors.

❑ Know how the Baby Boomer population is influencing the demands of products and services over the coming 25 years.

❑ Have a clear picture of what your ideal clientele looks like.

❑ Understand the differences between non-medical home care agency services and medical (home health) care agency services.

❑ Know the services a home care agency provides and the benefits it provides clients and their families.

❑ Understand the differences between an independently operated business, a franchise and buying an existing agency.

❑ Researched and decided how you'll start your entry to the home care industry: Independent, Franchise, Membership or Acquisition

❑ Read The E Myth by Michael Gerber.

❑ Understand the importance of creating and using systems in a business.

☐ Have a commitment to using systems in every aspect of your business.

If you need more information to improve your understanding of seniors, or to help in making decisions, consider researching each area in more depth to help you decide.

CHAPTER 3

RESEARCH AND ANALYZE YOUR MARKET

Market research is extremely important. Most of this research can be done online. If you can't find it online, go to your local public library or chamber of commerce. Visit your local senior center for senior specific information.

Another source of this information is senior home care franchise operations. Most of them have ready access to the following information or can get it quickly for your area.

Define Your Geographic Location, Size, and Population

For your business to be profitable and grow, you'll need to select the area of your service coverage carefully. Knowing the population of people ages 65 and older will help determine how much of an area you will need to cover to find the number of clients you aim to serve. Target the area(s) with a large and/or growing elder population and cities with large retirement communities.

Check the population census profiles around the city where you plan to provide service. Focus on the cities/communities that have the highest population of citizens age 65 and older. You can find this demographic information at www.census.gov, your local chamber of commerce, and your city/county economic development center.

Research the following:

❑ What is the population of the city(ies) you wish to provide services?

❑ Which city(ies) have the highest population of adults ages 65+?

❑ How big is the city/county/area that you wish to serve?
  You and your employees will be traveling to clients' homes. If you serve a large area, finding staff willing to travel and managing the staff becomes a consideration.

Identify Your Competition

Knowing your competition is an essential part of establishing your own business. The more you learn about them, the more you are able to clearly define how you'll distinguish yourself from them. Almost every area of your business can benefit by establishing a clear differentiation between you and competitors—services offered, the company logo, overall branding, marketing and ad campaigns, staffing strategies, and management.

Most communities have at least one company that provides in-home care services to the elderly population. Your job is to find who they are and learn all you can about them. Competition is easy to locate. Try looking in the following areas:

❖ Yellow Pages under "Home Health Care, Senior Services, Adult Care, Elder Care," etc.

❖ Online Yellow Pages under "Home Health Care, Senior Services, Adult Care, Elder Care," etc.

❖ Google "In Home Care, elder care, senior care" and add your city/county.

❖ Senior directories (often found at your community senior center or other senior care facilities).

❖ County Health Department Publications.

Now that you've found competition, make a list of your competitors and include the following:

☐ Name of each of your competitors.

☐ Competitors' locations.

☐ How long each has each been in business.

☐ The services they offer.

☐ What they charge.

☐ Whether they serve only seniors.

☐ Whether they are franchise units or independent.

☐ The areas they cover.

☐ Names of the owners.

☐ Their marketing tactics.

☐ Their website addresses?

Keep all the information you learn about your competition, and let it simmer. Look at their websites and see what they're doing. Call them, or have a friend or family member do this. As you perform your research activities, ask yourself, "How will my company will be different?" and begin to think of how you'll separate your company from the others. Awareness of competition keeps your eyes and ears open. When they're on your radar you'll recognize their logos, see their ads, and learn more about them.

There's no reason to approach competition as adversaries. You probably have a lot in common with them. In fact, you'll probably meet owners and managers from these companies as you attend community events. You can learn a lot from one another and may find that working with them can actually work to your benefit.

But not all agency owners and managers see competition this way. Some will view you as the enemy and see no reason to work together. They may even badmouth your company as they learn of competition entering the market. Commit to never speaking badly of your competitors. This is a business of people, and people talk. Saying bad things will reflect only on you. There is enough business for everyone, and if you approach your business with excellence, honesty, and ethics, competition will simply be another company specializing in the same field.

Determine Your Coverage Area

Is the population of seniors who may need home care large enough to be able to support your business? How many clients do you need?

The answer depends in part on a number of variables that you'll need to define:

❑ What are your overall goals for the business?

❑ What are your financial goals for the business?

❑ How much income do you want to make per month or per year?

❑ What are your target fixed expenses?

❑ Do you want to make this the largest senior home care company in your area?

❑ Do you simply want to have enough clients to achieve your financial goals?

If you don't know the answer to these questions now, don't worry. You'll define these in more detail as you develop your

Business Plan in Chapter 5. For now use a very conservative 1-2 percent as a rule of thumb.

Take the total number of seniors over age 65 years in your geographical area, and multiply that by 1 or 2 percent. Imagine that you are working with a population of 10,000 seniors over 65. Even with competition of four or five different agencies, each serving a conservative 2 percent of those, you could potentially serve between 100-200 clients (and growing as the Baby Boom population ages over the next 2-25 years).

State Laws and Licensing Requirements

Licensure requirements are a major step when planning your home care business. Every state carries different licensure regulations for home care agencies; you'll need to determine what requirements apply to your state and county. For example, Florida and New York require distinctive licenses for specific tasks of non-medical home care, whereas in California, the licensing for non-medical care requires a business license.

It's essential you're aware of and fully compliant with state laws before opening your doors. As you research the requirements, remember to explain that you're providing non-medical home care services; the regulations differ from those of a home health care agency. To find out which laws need to be followed in your state, contact the state health department and request a compliance kit. (These may be available online.) Following is the contact information needed for your state:

State Health Department Contacts

Alabama
Alabama Dept. of Human
Resources
Phone #: (334) 242-1310
www.dhr.state.al.us

Alaska
Alaska Dept. of Health and
Social Services
Phone #: (907) 465-3030
www.hss.state.ak.us

Arizona
Arizona Dept. of Economic
Security
Phone #: (602) 542-4791

www.de.state.az.us

Arkansas
Arkansas Dept. of Human
Services (ADHS)
Phone #: (501) 682-8650
www.arkansas.gov/dhhs/home
page.html

California
California Dept. of Social
Services
Phone #: (916) 455-6951
        and (916) 654-3345
www.dss.cahwnet.gov

Colorado
Colorado Dept. of Human
Services
Phone #: (303) 866-5700
        or 2-1-1
www.cdhs.state.co.us

Connecticut
Connecticut Dept. of Social
Services
Phone #: (800) 824-1508
www.ct.gov/dss/site/default.as
p

Delaware
Dept. of Health and Social
Services
Phone #: (302) 577-4502
www.dhss.delaware.gov/dhss

District of Columbia

D.C. Dept. of Human Services

Phone #: (202) 463-6211
www.dhs.dc.gov

Florida
Florida Agency for Health Care
Administration
Phone #: (850) 488-1295
www.fdhc.state.fl.us

Georgia
Georgia Dept. of Human
Resources
Phone #: (404) 651-6314
www.dhr.state.ga.us

Idaho
Idaho Dept. of Health and
Welfare
Phone #: (208) 334-6558
www.healthandwelfare.idaho.go
v

Indiana
Family and Social Services
Administration
Phone #: (317) 233-4690
www.in.gov/fssa

Kansas
Dept. of Social and
Rehabilitation Services
Phone #: (785) 296-3271
www.srskansas.org

Louisiana
Louisiana Dept. of Social
Services
Phone #: (225) 342-7475
www.dss.state.la.us

Maryland
Maryland Dept. of Human
Resources
Phone #: (800) 332-6347
  or local (410) 767-7109

www.dhr.state.md.us

Hawaii
Hawaii Dept. of Human Services

Phone #: (808) 586-4997
www.hawaii.gov/dhs

Illinois
Illinois Dept. of Human Services

Phone #: (217) 557-1601
www.dhs.state.il.us

Iowa
Iowa Dept. of Human Services

Phone #: (515) 281-3147
www.dhs.state.ia.us

Kentucky
Cabinet for Health and Family
Services
Phone #: (502) 564-7042
http://chfs.ky.gov

Maine
Maine Dept. of Health and
Human Services
Phone #: (207) 287-3707
www.maine.gov/dhhs

Massachusetts
Massachusetts Dept. of Social
Services
Phone #: (617) 748-2000
www.mass.gov/dss
Mass Office of Health and
Human Services
Phone #: (617) 727-7600

Michigan
Michigan Dept. of Community
Health
Phone #: (517) 373-3740
www.michigan.gov/mdch

Mississippi
Mississippi Dept. of Human
Services
Phone #: (800) 345-6347
or local (601) 359-4480
www.mdhs.state.ms.us

Montana
Montana Dept. of Public Health
and Human
Services
Phone #: (406) 444-5622
www.dphhs.mt.gov

Nevada
Nevada Dept. of Human
Resources
Phone #: (775) 687-4000
http://dhhs.nv.gov

New Jersey
NJ Dept. of Human Services

Phone #: (609) 292-5325
www.state.nj.us/humanservices

New York
NY State Dept. of Health
Office of Children & Family
Services
Phone #: (518) 474-5422
www.ocfs.state.ny.us

http://homecare.nyhealth.gov

Minnesota
Minnesota Dept. of Human
Services
Phone #: (651) 296-6117
www.dhs.state.mn.us

Missouri
Missouri Dept. of Social
Services
Phone #: 1-800-735-2466
or 1-573-751-4815
www.dss.mo.gov

Nebraska
Nebraska Health and Human
Services
System
Phone #: (402) 471-9433
www.hhs.state.ne.us

New Hampshire
NH Dept. of Health and Human
Services
Phone #: (603) 271-4685
www.dhhs.state.nh.us

New Mexico
NM Health & Human Services
Dept.
Phone #: (505) 827-7750
www.hsd.state.nm.us

North Carolina
N. Carolina Dept. of Health and
Human
Services
Phone #: (919) 733-4534
www.dhhs.state.nc.us

North Dakota
North Dakota Dept. of Human
Services
Phone #: (701) 328-2310
http://www.dhs.ri.gov

Oklahoma
Oklahoma Dept. of Human
Services

Phone #: (405) 521-3646

www.okdhs.org

Pennsylvania
Pennsylvania Dept. of Public
Welfare (DPW)
Phone #: (717) 787-2600
www.dpw.state.pa.us/ServicesP
rograms

South Carolina
SC Dept. of Health and Human
Services
Phone #: (803) 898-2500
www.state.sc.us/dss
South Carolina Dept. of Social
Services
Phone #: (803) 898-7601

Texas
Health and Human Services
Commission
www.hhsc.state.tx.us
Phone #: (512) 424-6500

Ohio
Ohio Dept. of Job and Family
Services
Phone #: (614) 466-6282
http://jfs.ohio.gov

Oregon
Oregon Dept. of Human
Services
Phone #: (800) 422-6012
         or local (503) 945-5944
www.oregon.gov/DHS/index.sht
ml

Rhode Island
Rhode Island Dept. of Human
Services
Phone #: (401) 462-2121
www.dhs.state.ri.us

Tennessee
Tennessee Dept. of Human
Services
Phone #: (615) 313-4707
www.state.tn.us/humanserv

Utah
Utah Dept. of Health

Phone #: (801) 538-6101
www.health.state.ut.us
Utah Dept. of Human Services
Phone #: (801) 538-4001
www.dhs.state.ut.us

Vermont
Vermont Agency of Human
Services
Phone #: (802) 241-2220
www.ahs.state.vt.us

Washington
WA Dept. of Social and Health
Services
Phone #: (360) 902-7800
www1.dshs.wa.gov

Wisconsin
WI Dept. of Health and Family
Services
Phone #: (608) 266-9622

www.dhfs.state.wi.us

Virginia
Dept. of Medical Assistance
Services
Phone #: (804) 786-7933
www.dmas.virginia.gov
Virginia Dept. of Social Services
Phone #: (804) 692-1901
www.dss.state.va.us

West Virginia
WV Dept. of Health and Human
Resources
Phone #: (304) 558-0684
www.wvdhhr.org

Wyoming
Wyoming Dept. of Health

Phone #: (307) 777-7656
http://wdh.state.wy.us/main/i
ndex.asp

Chapter 3 review Task List

Upon completing Chapter 3 you should have:

☐ A clear knowledge of your service area's region and demographic.

☐ Defined the geographic area your company will serve.

☐ A demographic figure of how many seniors are in your service area.

☐ Created a list of and know about each of your competitors.

☐ Called your competitors and learned about their rates and niche.

☐ A complete understanding of your state's licensure requirements

☐ Contacted your state's health department for details of licensure compliance requirements.

☐ Created a 'to-do" list to become compliant with state licensing requirements.

☐ Completed all the tasks necessary to become compliant with state licensure.

CHAPTER 4

SETTING UP YOUR BUSINESS

Setting up your business involves some tedious (even boring) tasks. But accomplishing these tasks is essential. If you don't address these in the beginning, the reality of their necessity will return to remind you in ways that cost you money, time, or both.

These tasks don't consume large amounts of time or effort, and individually they are rather simple. Stay focused, and take immediate action on each step in this chapter so you'll be prepared for promptly generating revenue. You'll also enjoy a significant amount of accomplishment. Make a commitment to yourself *right now* to complete all the tasks included in setting up your business before moving to the next steps.

Legal Entity Setup

One of the first and most important business decisions you'll have to make is the type of business entity to operate under. Consider all the options, and choose the one that best fits your situation.

Each type of entity has advantages and disadvantages. The type you choose will determine and affect your tax filing requirements, personal risk exposure, insurance requirements, and more. It's highly recommended that you consult with your attorney and tax accountant to help you decide which entity to choose. Each individual's situation is different, so make sure you have a thorough understanding of the differences and how each one benefits you from a legal and financial perspective.

Provided in this chapter are brief overviews of what each entity is with links to the IRS website that give more details. The most common forms of business used today are:

- ❖ Sole Proprietorship

- ❖ Partnership

- ❖ C Corporation

- ❖ S Corporation

- ❖ LLC (Limited Liability Company)

Sole Proprietorship

The sole proprietorship is typically used if you're the sole owner of an unincorporated business. This entity has the easiest form of entry; however, it carries the least amount of legal protection for your assets. Essentially, the sole proprietorship entity is a business that operates under your personal social security number; your business name is filed simply as a DBA (Doing Business As) with your county.

Since the business is operated using your personal SSN, sole proprietorships taxes are reported annually through the IRS 1040 Form. More information about the IRS requirements for sole proprietorship can be found here:

http://www.irs.gov/businesses/small/article/0,,id=98202,00.html

Partnership

Partnership entities are typically formed when two or more people join together to own a business. Each person, or partner, brings something of value to the arrangement in the formation and execution of the business. Most commonly this value includes capital, skills, property, or labor.

Partnerships are reported annually through the IRS Form 1065. More information about the IRS requirements for partnership can be found here:

http://www.irs.gov/businesses/small/article/0,,id=98214,00.html

54

C Corporation

The C corporation comprises shareholders who, in exchange for capital, skills, property, or labor, are issued corporation capital stock. The C Corporation provides the same tax deduction benefits as a sole proprietorship in calculating its taxable income; however, it's recognized as a separate taxpaying entity by the federal IRS. It's also often referred to as a double taxation entity because profits are taxed to the corporation when earned, and shareholders are also taxed when the profits are distributed as dividends. Accounting and tax preparation costs are also considerably higher than a simple sole proprietorship.

C corporations are reported annually through the IRS Form 1120. Find more detailed information about the IRS requirements here:

http://www.irs.gov/businesses/small/article/0,,id=98240,00.html

S Corporation

The S corporation provides much of the same legal benefits and protections as a c Corporation without the double taxation burden. The S corporation has some restrictions, including 100 or fewer shareholders, only one class of stock, and not being a financial institution, insurance company, or an international sales corporation.

To become an S corporation, the corporation needs to file a Form 2553 Election by a Small Business Corporation signed by all shareholders of the corporation after the initial formation of the corporation and within a specific period.

S corporations are reported annually through the IRS Form 1120S with the shareholders reporting the income on their personal tax returns and assessed at the tax rates of each individual shareholder's income tax rates. More information about the IRS requirements for an S corporation can be found here:

http://www.irs.gov/businesses/small/article/0,,id=98263,00.html

LLC (Limited Liability Company)

The limited liability company (LLC), the newest entity form, has become popular because owners have a limited personal liability for the debts and actions of the LLC, its similarity to a partnership by offering flexibility of management, and the pass-through taxation benefit. Owners of the LLC are not shareholders; they are members that can include individuals, corporations, other LLCs and foreign entities. There are single member LLCs and multiple member LLCs; understanding the differences are important.

LLCs report annually through the IRS Form 8832 with the shareholders reporting the income on their personal tax returns and assessed at the tax rates of each individual shareholder's income tax rates. More information about the IRS requirements of LLCs can be found here: http://www.irs.gov/businesses/small/article/0,,id=98277,00.html

The process to establish your legal entity is all about correctly filing proper paperwork. There are several ways to accomplish this:

Web Based Incorporating Services

The Company Corporation
www.incorporate.com

Legal Zoom
www.legalzoom.com

My Corporation
www.mycorporation.com

My New Company
www.mynewcompany.com

56

1. *Your attorney can help you.*

When you are being advised of what type of entity to choose, ask how much they charge to set up the entity—lawyers often are more expensive than other available sources to accomplish the same result. Depending on your situation, however, having your attorney draft the paperwork to accommodate your situation specifically may be worth your peace of mind over the cost.

2. *Hire a local or web based firm that specializes specifically in these services.*

They're often less expensive, they specialize in forming company entities, they know the requirements for each state, and you can do all the work from your computer while they walk you through the process step by step.

Whether your attorney helps you or whether you use Internet based services, the process is the same, and the result will be similar.

The web based services will usually do a corporate name search and file for an EIN for you, though if you're prepared in advance you'll already know. If you choose to use a web based service, read and do the next three sections first. Doing so could save you a few dollars if you wish to do the easy tasks yourself.

Choose Your Business Name

What's in a name? A lot! Your company's name can work for or against you, so put considerable thought into the name. A name itself can instantly differentiate you from competition. The name should bring you and others positive connotations and tell people what you do.

As you begin thinking about what name would fit your company, consider some of the following tips:

❖ Consider a short, easy to pronounce, memorable name.

❖ The terms "home care," "senior care," "elder care," "at home," etc. tell people right away what your business does.

❖ Geographical names (e.g., Santa Barbara Home Care) limit growth if the company grows beyond the area.

❖ Reference a words origin, translation or meaning to a word.

❖ A name starting with an A will put you in the beginning of phone books, referral lists, directories, etc.

❖ People remember certain types of unusual names; however, make sure that the name isn't so unusual or cheesy that it creates a poor first impression.

❖ Think about how you'd like people to feel when they hear the name.

❖ When thinking up a company name, come up with at least 10 alternatives. If that sounds difficult, don't worry; the brainstorming exercise below will help you.

You'll need to make sure the name is still available for you to use. With the list of 10 names in order of preference, you have a solid start at obtaining a name you want. Before you can begin using the name, you must complete a series of checks or searches and register the name.

BRAINSTORM YOUR COMPANY NAME
EXERCISE

Take out a piece of paper and for the next 15 – 20 minutes brainstorm as many names as come to mind. Don't judge whether they sound good. Silly, corny, or obnoxious ideas can all spark other ideas. You'll weed out ones you don't like later. Play with different words, combinations, or even partial words.

1. Review your list with a friend, and ask for his or her reaction to each one.

2. Think about how each name makes you feel. The name should make you and others feel good.

3. Weed out the names that you're certain won't work or don't feel good.

4. Place a priority to the ones remaining, with no less than 10 finalists. If you don't have 10, go back to step 1.

Verify Trademarks

Check to ensure that no one has trademarked your chosen name or is currently using it within your state. If you opted to have an attorney or web service set up your entity for you, the name search may already be included in the fee. If it isn't or you're not sure, call and ask them to include it.

The two levels you should check are federal and state level:

❑ The Federal Trademark office

❑ Your Secretary of State

To check if your desired name has been registered as an official trademark, search the federal trademark office database here: www.uspto.gov/trademarks/index.jsp. If the name is used in a different state, you might still be able to use it. If a corporation decides to get persnickety and has registered it as a trademark on the federal level, you could find yourself in a legal battle or be forced to change your name altogether.

If you're planning to go nationwide or have a large statewide presence, consider filing your own name with the federal trademark office. A U.S. trademark or service mark is about $325—a small fee compared to costs of defending it in courts. If you're planning to maintain a small local business, this is not necessary.

Corporate Business Name Search

If you've elected a partnership, corporation, or LLC, check with your Secretary of State's database to ensure the name you'd like hasn't already been assigned or trademarked. Select a name that isn't already in use in your state, and if you intend to go national, consider a name that isn't nationally taken or you may find yourself in an unwanted legal battle down the road and having to rename the company. Fortunately, most states provide free access to their databases through the web for corporate name searches.

If your name search reveals that your chosen name has already been taken, select the second name, and so on until one is available. Once you've verified that your name is available, request or download the forms necessary, and register your name immediately.

Obtain a Fictitious Business Name Statement

A fictitious business name (FBN), or DBA (doing business as) allows you to do business under a specific business name legally with very little cost and without having to create a new business entity. A FBN allows you to legally advertise, accept payment, operate and represent yourself under the FBN name. Presenting your business under a name other than yourself or your entity name (i.e., a sole proprietorship or a name different from your legal entity name) without an FBN can be considered fraud.

In most cases, you'll want to have a FBN if you choose to operate as a sole proprietorship entity that differs from your own name. Obtaining a FBN is so inexpensive and simple that there really is no excuse to not file for one.

The FBN also allows for a single entity (i.e., Partnership, LLC, Corporation) to operate numerous businesses without creating a separate legal entity for each business. For example, if you already have a corporation named The Smith Corporation and want to operate your home care company within that corporation, then file for a FBN as "Smith's Lovely Home Care Services."

Some states require that you register your FBN with the Secretary of State; however, in most states the FBN is handled at the county level. The fees, forms, and processes differ among counties.

To learn what your county requires, Google "Fictitious Business Name in (your county, state)" or "Clerk Recorder Office (your county, state) Fictitious Business Name." Contact them for the details. Although many counties have streamlined this process through a website, some haven't, so a trip to the County Recorders Office may be necessary.

The process generally requires you do a search through their database to ensure the name you'd like isn't taken already. You'll submit a form along with the filing fee (which is usually between $10 and $75). Depending on your county requirements, you may need to publish a notice in your local newspaper and show legal proof from the publication that the requirement was met.

Check Domain Names

Now that you've got a legally registered name, find the domain name for your company. This will require searching the master Internet database as well. If you already know who will be creating your website, contact them to help you. Work with them to select a name or follow some of the following suggestions.

The greatest challenge in selecting your domain name is finding one that's available. Common domain names may already be taken, so if you have a unique business name chances are greater you'll get a good one you like. Select one that's not too long, is easy to spell, and easy to remember. Be creative, and try putting different words together, abbreviate, or use the first letters of the company name.

Find a Good Domain Name

To help you think of an available domain name that fits your company, try the following tools:

Bust-A-Name
www.bustaname.com

Domain Tools
www.domaintools.com

Once you've found an available domain name, you'll need to register it. Both the above tools will allow you to register the domain name(s) you select; however, you'll still need to create and host the site.

Build and Host Your Website

Domain name purchase and build-your-website as all-in-one package solutions:

Go Daddy
www.godaddy.com

Network Solutions
www.networksolutions.com

Intuit
www.intuit.com

Newtek Web Hosting
www.crystaltech.com

Obtain Your EIN

The IRS requires any business that hires employees to have an EIN (Employer Identification Number. The EIN number is easy to obtain, and you can apply for it online directly through the IRS Website at http://www.irs.gov/businesses/small/article/0,,id=102767,00.html). If you used one of the online entity formation companies recommended earlier and selected the option for them to obtain, then you may have already done this step.

After you've completed the online application, you'll be issued an EIN number immediately with a document to print for proof. Save that PDF document for future use.

Create Your Logo

The company title is more than just a cool-looking piece of graphic art. A quality logo is well thought out; it integrates graphics, character fonts, and art to create a memorable representation and statement about your company. The logo becomes the foundation of all your branding efforts, including your business cards, website, letterheads, envelopes, advertising, employee representation, and more.

Need a Logo Designed?

Two online companies recommended for great service experience, fair pricing, and excellent results:

99 Dollar Logos - www.99dollarlogos.com.
Very professional and has been creating logos and branding for years!

Logo Design Guru - www.logodesignguru.com.
Easy to work with and provides many services beyond logo design.

If you're not a graphic artist or haven't created logos in the past, outsource this step. Some graphic artists specialize in logos and can create one relatively quickly and inexpensively—often under $300.

When creating your logo, keep these basic guidelines in mind:

- ❖ The logo should be memorable and grab attention in just a few seconds.

- ❖ Keep the logo simple—less is more.

- ❖ Make the logo scalable—readable at an inch high or as big as a billboard.

- ❖ Limit the colors, and choose them carefully.

- ❖ The logo should be describable.

- ❖ Be unique—don't mimic your competition's logo; stand out.

❖ The logo does not have to be a symbol of what your company does.

❖ Don't use stock art or photos in a logo. These are costly and often involve legal infringements.

As you envision your logo, consider some of the nation's largest companies—McDonalds, FedEx, Nike, HP, Ford, Bank of America, etc. Their logos are all quite simple, grab attention quickly, and are memorable. Note that most of them use only one or two colors. Ongoing printing costs balloon with every color you add to the logo, and those costs will grow exponentially as the company grows.

Designers are ubiquitous, locally and online. Working with local designers allows you to work with them face to face and support your local small business community. To find one online, Google "logo designers."

As you research different designers, ask questions about their design process, how many proofs you'll be able to choose from, how many revisions can be made, how the completed logos are delivered, and what all costs are upfront. Ask for examples of their work, and talk to their existing clients. This is your brand you'll be exposing to the world, so take your time and consider carefully.

Completing State Licensure Requirements

By now you should have received the information from your State Health Department outlining the licensure requirements discussed in Chapter 3: State Laws and Licensing Requirements. If you haven't completed all the steps required by your state, update the task list, and make sure you're on track to complete all the requirements.

Prepare Your Office

Building your business requires an office space from which to operate your business. If you haven't begun to think about your office yet, now is the time. Even if you already have an office space, this portion may contain suggestions you haven't thought of yet.

In general, you have two choices for an office. Your available start-up capital often makes this decision for you:

1. Rent/lease an office space from the start.

2. Establish a home office.

Renting/Leasing and Office Space

Leasing a business office can affect your profitability, employee morale, and your ability to grow right from the beginning. If you lease an office from the start, make sure you have enough start-up capital to provide a minimum of 12 months of lease payments in addition to your operating expenses. This may sound excessive; however, remember that one of the most common reasons businesses fail in the first few years is lack of capital—i.e., running out of it too quickly.

Before you begin looking at space, assemble a team to help you, including a local real estate attorney and a commercial real estate agent. Leasing commercial office space is quite different than leasing an apartment or residential home, and they can help you through this process. Negotiating leases for an office space involves many terms and conditions, and trying to do it alone can be daunting. A team who specializes in commercial real estate contracts and knows your area well will make this process much easier.

If your startup funds allow for an outside office, that's terrific! Such an office is an official business location and a professional presence. It's separate from your home, and if you have children, you'll be more effective and productive while there.

Start with a small office; you won't need a lot of room to begin. A common mistake is leasing a too-large space with the intention of "growing into it." It's better to grow out of your space and need more room than to have so much room that you risk growing out of business altogether by being unable to support the overhead. Location is important, but you don't need prime downtown space. Your office should be easy for employees and occasional potential clients to find. (Usually you will meet clients in their own homes.)

Consider a business incubator office rental if your city has one. These incubator offices are small office units shared by other entrepreneurs within the same building at significantly reduced rates. See www.nbia.org to find if one is available in your area. These office spaces come in different sizes and often include a phone, Internet, a conference room, a receptionist, and a lobby for a reasonably low price. Some have copy machines and many other ala carte services that can help a small business look professional for an inexpensive rate. You may find yourself sharing expertise in various areas as well.

Another cost-reducing approach is sharing an office with another company, possibly one that even complements your home care agency.

Home Office

Home offices carry benefits as well. Obviously, they're very convenient. I've coached numerous owners who sprouted their home care agency from a home based office and eventually grew into an office space as the business supported the overhead expense.

Home care is a non-stop business, especially as you grow. Because you will provide services 24 hours a day, you receive phone calls late at night; having the office at home allows you to handle situations immediately. You're also able to schedule your day flexibly and accomplish the tasks at the times most efficient for you without having to travel to an office.

The cost savings of a home office are significant, which allows you to conserve capital as you grow your business. You're able to invest your funds in growing your client base and generating the revenue to support a formal office. From a tax perspective, the home office tax deduction is available to you, though consult your tax attorney for this benefit. From a strictly profit and loss standpoint, a home office is a good choice.

Working from your home office does require some creativity and self discipline, however. For example, you'll need to meet and interview applicants, conduct staff reviews, and hold staff meetings; occasionally a family may wish to meet you outside their parents' home. Solutions include meeting in coffee houses or meeting rooms in libraries, your local chamber of commerce, town hall, churches, employment centers, unemployment offices, workforce centers, and senior centers.

It's not recommended that you purchase a building at this point; you'll initially lack the cash flow to pay for it and will be burdened with the debt to carry it early on. Wait until your revenues can justify it.

The following page summarizes Pros and Cons of your office options.

Pros and Cons of Leased Office and Home Office

LEASED OFFICE	HOME OFFICE
PROS	**PROS**
• Dedicated work space away from home.	• Significant cost savings compared with leasing an office.
• Professional location for meeting applicants and possible clients.	• Convenient, shorter commute.
• Higher productivity with work/home separation.	• Flexible work schedule.
CONS	• Home-office tax deduction = more cost savings.
• Requires significant up-front capital.	**CONS**
• Lengthy commitments to the landlord.	• Easy to procrastinate work with all the home activities crying for your attention.
• Commute time is often inconvenient—e.g., if you need access to files at midnight, you need to go to the office.	• Space to grow is often limited.
• Solitude is quickly felt when just starting out and you're alone in the office.	• Separating work from personal time may quickly turn you into a workaholic.
• Fewer amenities than home when renting lower cost office space to save money.	• Separating family time from work time is often difficult for kids or spouses to understand. If you're home, they see you as available, even if you're working.

Office Tools Needed:

Now that you've determined where your office will be located, you'll need tools to get started.

- ❏ A computer—preferably a laptop, though a desktop will work initially. The computer should be no older than two or three years.

- ❏ High speed Internet connection. Dial-up won't cut it.

- ❏ Telephone. Obtain a phone number that you'll use solely for business. It should be a local number. A cell phone works great initially.

- ❏ Five-subject notebook. As you think of things related to your business, jot them down. Five-subject notebooks work well for keeping organized.

- ❏ Computer desk and chair.

- ❏ File cabinet.

- ❏ Printer—preferably an "all in one" (copy/scan/fax/print), which are inexpensive these days,

- ❏ Fax machine (if not included with the printer)

- ❏ Copy machine (if not included with the printer). A small copy machine will suffice at this point.

You'll need basic office supplies as well.

- ❏ File folders

- ❏ Pens and pencils

- ❏ Stapler and staples

- ❏ Paper clips

- ❏ Calculator

- ☐ Copy/printer paper and higher grade printer presentation paper
- ☐ 20-30 three-ring binders
- ☐ Bi-Fold Folders

Create business cards and brochures

Once your logo is designed you can begin putting it to work by creating your business cards and brochures. On the Internet you can find many companies that allow you upload your logo and content to existing templates and design the print items yourself. The upside is that you can create business cards, brochures, letterheads, envelopes, and more within a few hours. The downside is that your options are limited to the templates they provide.

If you'd prefer a more original card and brochure, consult a graphics professional. Such professionals do this work for a living and can create materials in a fraction of the time that it would take you.

As you work with a graphic designer, keep in mind that what you're doing is building your branding image—which starts with the logo. The logo's look, feel, and colors should carry through to the business cards, brochure, website, and any print material that leaves your office.

Create Your Business Cards & Brochures

Consider these online design and print houses that help you design and print your business cards, brochures, letterheads, and more.

Vista Print
www.vistaprint.com.

Sharp Dots
www.sharpdots.com.

Uprinting
www.uprinting.com.

Chapter 4 Review Task List

Upon completing Chapter 4 you should have:

☐ Decided on the legal entity of your business.

☐ Filed the legal documents to create your business entity.

☐ Chosen your business name.

☐ Verified that the business name is legally available.

☐ Registered the business name.

☐ Obtained your EIN.

☐ Filed proper documents to meet state licensure requirements.

☐ Purchased a domain name.

☐ Purchased office tools and equipment.

☐ Set up your office.

☐ Created a logo with overall branding look and feel.

CHAPTER 5

CREATE YOUR BUSINESS PLAN

A solid business plan is a vital component to starting and growing your business. You wouldn't build a house without careful planning; you create a blueprint so that builders know how to make the vision a reality. Put the same planning into your business plan. Even if you use the business plan only for guidance, it will help keep you focused and help you succeed.

Many people are afraid of the business plan. They think it needs to be a 100-page document with a bunch of gibberish. On the contrary, it should be clear and concise enough to outline what you want your business to look like in 1 year, 5 years, and 10 years. It's a fluid document that, like a blueprint, gives you direction to build your vision. Your plan will change as new opportunities present themselves, and that's okay. Unless you'll be seeking investors for capital and need a formal plan, your plan needs to make sense only to you and your partner(s) and key management personnel. It works best to keep it simple while thinking through the areas that are essential to your business.

Hundreds of books have been written about business plans, and countless resources are available online to help you create one. There are many formats and styles to creating a business plan.

Investing in a business plan software program can simplify the process of creating a plan as simple or complex as you wish. One that stands far above the rest for its ease of use and simplicity to create is Business Plan Pro by Palo Alto Software. The software asks you a series of questions and generates a business plan based on your answers, You still must clearly think through your vision; however, the process of writing the plan is less daunting. Find it from Amazon here.

Business Plan Outline

The following basic business plan outline can be used as a guide to get your plan created. This simple outline covers the essential areas to consider and provides a foundation of what your business plan should include. The outline and a business plan template are available for download at the book's website.

I. The Company
   a. Vision and Mission Statement
   b. Description of Business
   c. Target Market and Customers
   d. Growth Trends in This Business
   e. The Vision and People Involved
   f. Risks

II. Business Organization
   a. Management Team
   b. Board of Directors
   c. Employees
   d. Location
   e. Licenses and Permits

III. Competitive Analysis
   a. Competition
   b. Competitive Differentiation

IV. Services/Products
   a. Services Offered
   b. Future Services/Products
   c. Service Delivery and Support

V. Marketing and Sales
   a. Marketing Plan
   b. Sales Strategy
   c. Sales Cycle
   d. Pricing Model and Strategy
   e. Marketing Channels
   f. Strategic Alliances/Relationships

VI. Finance
   a. Financial Summary
   b. Revenue Sources

      c.   Funding Requirements

      d.   Income Projections

      e.   Cash Flow Projections

      f.   Balance Sheet Projections

This business plan outline (one among many) includes the important elements of a basic plan. This particular outline is designed for the home care business, to be viewed by you, your partners, and the management team. It's easy to follow and create. If you're seeking investor capital, plan to invest considerable more time and effort into a far more comprehensive plan and seek professional guidance to meet potential investors' expectations and general requirements.

Financial Planning and Projections

The finance section is one of the most important pieces of your business plan. Without planning the use of existing money and future revenues (cash flow) it's difficult to grow a business.

Know and Understand Your Cash Flow

Cash flow is the blood of any business. Following the basic rules of cash flow will enable you to create the business you envision. Ignoring them will kill your business.

1. **Cash is king.** Cash keeps your business alive. Without cash, your business is dead.

2. **Always have cash.** Commit to doing whatever it takes to not run out.

3. **Always know the exact current cash balance.** Not knowing will affect your decisions and can sink you.

4. **Keep up with your bookkeeping.** Falling behind on your bookkeeping will give you false balances. (Not good.)

5. **Get it done.** If you don't have the time to do the work to know the balance, hire someone to do it for you.

6. **Manage from your books, not your bank balance.** If your books are up to date, you'll know your exact cash position at all times.

7. **Project your cash flow six months in advance.** This is essential to making informed, profitable business decisions.

8. **Cash problems are preventable.** Projecting your cash flow six months in advance will help foresee problems and address them early.

Break-Even Projection

A break-even projection, also known as a cash flow projection, is essentially a budget detailing all projected income and expenses over the coming 6 to 12 months, combined with your existing investment capital; it identifies when your business has enough revenue to be self supporting—i.e., when it breaks even. It considers projected sales revenue, capital expenditures such as office equipment, and the living expenses you'll incur while building the new business.

Do not skip this step! Countless businesses fail because they just wing it and then run out of cash sooner than they thought. Knowing and understanding your cash flow position each month allows you to plan and adjust your expenditures so there's always enough cash on hand.

The following spreadsheet is an example of a simple break-even projection. In the example, $30K of upfront capital is available; the break-even point comes at the end of month 3 with $8,375 of the startup funds still available. Download an editable version of the Break Even Projection from the website.

Break Even Projections 6 Months

	Month 1	Month 2	Month 3	Month 4	Month 5	Month 6	Total
Beginning Cash on Hand	$30,000	$17,135	$10,470	$8,375	$9,940	$14,895	$30,000
Gross Revenue:							
Companion Care		3,000	5,000	8,000	11,500	15,000	42,500
Deposits		1,500	3,000	5,000	6,500	8,500	24,500
Total Revenue	-	4,500	8,000	13,000	18,000	23,500	67,000
Cost of Sales:							
60%		1,800	3,000	4,800	6,900	9,000	25,500
Other 1							-
Total Cost of Sales	-	1,800	3,000	4,800	6,900	9,000	25,500
Gross Profit	-	2,700	5,000	8,200	11,100	14,500	41,500
Fixed Operating Expenses:							
Ads - (Senior directory, Yellow Pgs)	350	350	350	350	350	350	2,100
Phone & cell phones	150	150	150	150	150	150	900
Utilities	45	45	45	45	45	45	270
Rent	500	500	500	500	500	500	3,000
Other 1							-
Total Fixed Expenses	1,045	1,045	1,045	1,045	1,045	1,045	6,270
Variable Operating Expenses:							
Marketing (business cards, brochures, brand)	2,100	2,000	1,900	1,500	1,000	1,000	9,500
Ads (Employment Ads)	350	300	250	300	300	225	1,725
Vehicles/Transportation	120	100	130	120	100	140	710
Office Tools (Computer, Printer, etc)	3,500	85	110	135	150	160	4,140
Payroll Services		85	110	135	150	160	640
Professional Development							-
Outsourced Services	2,500	2,500	300	150	150	150	5,750
Other 1							-
Total Variable Expenses	8,570	5,070	2,800	2,340	1,850	1,835	22,465
TOTALS:							
Total Operating Expenses	9,615	6,115	3,845	3,385	2,895	2,880	28,735
Net Cash Flow	(9,615)	(3,415)	1,155	4,815	8,205	11,620	12,765
Personal Living Expenses	3,250	3,250	3,250	3,250	3,250	3,250	3,250
Ending Cash Balance	$17,135	$10,470	$8,375	$9,940	$14,895	$23,265	$39,515

Chapter 5 Review Task List

Upon completing Chapter 5, you should have:

❑ Given clear thought to what your business will look in 1 year, 3 years, and 10 years.

❑ Clearly visualized your business at 1 year, 3 years, and 10 years.

❑ Downloaded a business plan template or purchased business plan software.

❑ Created your business plan.

❑ Completed your financial projections and cash flow analysis.

❑ A good understanding of cash flow projections.

❑ Created a Break Even Projection and know your estimated break-even timeline.

CHAPTER 6

PREPARE OPERATIONS SYSTEMS

Your business will operate best if you have systems in place from the start. Avoid being a slave to your business, never able to take time off, and having your business run you. Since you've begun reading, or hopefully finished *EMyth,* the concept of systems should make complete sense.

Create Your Files System

Creating an organized file system will save you time, frustration, and energy. You'll know where to locate things and, most importantly you'll be able to teach new staff a consistent system,

As you create your file systems, think beyond what you yourself can understand. At some point you'll hand the task to staff. Consistency in systems will save time and energy when it's time to file things or locate the files in the future. As the business grows it's much more difficult to rearrange or recreate a file system.

Your file system should include both the physical files that are stored in your file cabinet as well as your computerized filing system. Create consistency between the two types early on. Consider striving for an office system that's as paper-free as possible. The more you can streamline your files into the digital format, the more autonomous the office can run, the more easily you can access needed information, and the fewer staff members you'll need to manage the information.

If you have a filing system that works for you and is easily taught to others, use it. Consider creating sections and folders outlined below. The list isn't exhaustive, so plan that your file system will grow it as your business expands.

Accounting	Marketing
Accounts Receivable (Invoices and Deposits)	Brochure Design
	Competition
Accounts Payable (Bills)	Logo Design
Bank Statements	Marketing Goals
Insurance	Marketing Ideas
Merchant Account Statements	Marketing Sources
Payroll	Marketing Tracking
Purchase Receipts	
	Office Administration
Human Resources	Administrative Forms
Applicants	Brochure
Applicants Interviewed	Letterhead
Employee	Phone Scripts
Employees – Former	Policies & Procedures
HR Goals	
Staff Review Forms	Sales
Training	Clients
	Lead Sources
Operations	Sales Contracts
Operations Forms	Sales Forms
Operations Goals	
Operations Reports	

It's not essential to be computer savvy or up on the latest technology. It would benefit you greatly to learn, however, as your competition will be, and such knowledge will save you time.

The Internet has spawned new technology called the "cloud" network—a network that is not location specific. Company information is placed on secure servers that are accessible via the Internet instead of solely from your office computer. This allows you to access the information from your computer whenever you have internet access. This technology is secure and inexpensive—even free, in many cases.

Google, for example, is more than a search engine. It has evolved into a company that provides tools that support, encourage, and help small business owners. One free service is called Google Docs. http://docs.google.com. Needing only a user account, you can upload Microsoft Word, Excel, and PowerPoint documents, Adobe PDF, OpenDocuments, and photos to your account and make them available to those you wish. These chosen users can view and update the documents, which are stored on secure Google servers—effectively creating a cloud network for your company.

How can a cloud network help you? If your schedule includes a day full of assessment appointments, the information you gather about a client traditionally doesn't get back to the office until you do. Office staff can't begin the process of staffing a new client until you get the information back to them. When the information is securely available anywhere, anytime from the internet, your staff can see it as soon as you complete an assessment. They can start working to schedule staff to fulfill the client's needs while you're off to your next appointment.

For another example, place articles, forms, or marketing material in this location. As you talk with prospective clients or referral sources, it may occur to you that they would benefit from a specific document or article . You can email it to them immediately. Very basic examples, yet uses of this capability are endless. By using vendors that provide web based services essentially allows your company to operate within a cloud network. Centralized to anywhere you are.

Prepare Your Forms

For systems to be useful and effective they need to have consistency and be duplicatable for every person using the system. Forms make this possible.

You can use the forms as they are presented or make modifications to fit your specific business needs.

Employee Forms

- ❑ Application for Employment (if you use paper application process)
- ❑ Applicant Interview Assessment
- ❑ Applicant Checklist
- ❑ Applicant Reference Check Forms
- ❑ Past Employers/Business References
- ❑ Personal References
- ❑ Employment Eligibility Form (Dept of Justice I-9 Form)
- ❑ Taxes Withholding Form (IRS W-4 Form)
- ❑ Missing Employment Documents Request
- ❑ Employee Welcome Letter
- ❑ Employment Contract Agreement
- ❑ Policies and Procedures Manual
- ❑ Care Plan Visit Documentation Logs
- ❑ Gift Policy Acknowledgement Agreement
- ❑ Key Policy Acknowledgement Agreement
- ❑ Employee Review and Checklist

Sales – Client Acquisition Forms

- ☐ Prospect Inquiry Form (PIF)
- ☐ Client Assessment Forms
- ☐ Home Care Service Contracts
- ☐ Client Care Plans
- ☐ Client Expectation Letters
- ☐ Client Handbooks
- ☐ Supervisory Follow-Up Visit Checklist
- ☐ Home Safety Checklists

Download forms at www.homecarehowto.com. After downloading the forms, make copies. Start with 10 to 30 copies of each form.

Prepare Prospect Information Packs (PIPs)

When you receive inquiries, you'll be asked for more information about your services. The "sales" process of in-home care can range from a day to over a year, It's a big step for many seniors to admit they need help, another step to accept the help, and yet another step to be open to the idea of someone other than family helping them in their home. A phone call will go only so far—you want to provide potential clients with information that will keep you first in mind when they are ready to accept the help they need.

A PIP—or prospect information pack—will help you do just that. A PIP will provide the information necessary to help educate the prospect—whether it's the potential client or his or her spouse, children, family, or friends.

A PIP should include the following:

- [ ] A personalized welcome letter
- [ ] Your company brochure (template available on website)
- [ ] Business card(s)
- [ ] Testimonials
- [ ] List of services
- [ ] List of service pricing
- [ ] Press releases
- [ ] Articles that coincide with the type of situation the potential client is currently dealing with
- [ ] Company branded folder
- [ ] A branded folder holds all this information in a clean, well packaged manner. You could have folders printed specifically for this purpose or create your own by labeling generic folders with your logo and tag line.

Set up Contact Management System

As you receive inquiries from prospective clients, employee applicants, and referral sources, you must track these names and contact information. Furthermore, as your organization grows keeping track of your conversations with clients, vendors, employees and any other contact becomes more challenging. So keeping track of your interactions from first meeting throughout the relationship is essential.

Many software programs are designed specifically as out-of-the-box contact management programs (CRM)—don't waste time trying to create your own. CRM programs organize, store, and make available all your communication with clients, meetings, email, phone calls, and more. They can also help greatly in acquiring new clients.

As you choose a CRM keep in mind that it's the program you'll probably stay with for a while as it's difficult to just change the system after you've used it a while. Databases often carry proprietary formats and are purposely incompatible with competitors' systems. Find the program that works best for your business.

There are two approaches to the contact management system:

1. Use a separate CRM designed specifically for that one purpose — contact management.
2. Use a CRM system that is already integrated to your other business operations systems to reduce redundant data entry and improve reporting capabilities.

Separate CRMs

Many comprehensive and useful software programs are available for separate stand-alone CRMs. The stand-alone programs operate on a separate database, so using one will require double or triple entry of the contact's name into the other databases that manage your client and care provider schedules.

The following separate CRMs have proven to be excellent tools:

ACT!—www.act.com
Client based software CRM that runs on your computer. The corporate edition also allows for accessing the information via the web (at additional cost).

Sales Force—www.salesforce.com/CRM
A web based subscription service. It's available anywhere, anytime, putting your CRM in the cloud network.

Zoho—www.zoho.com
Another web based subscription CRM service; it's free for

three users with some limitations. An inexpensive way to begin with capability to add features while growing.

Integrated CRMs

Double entry can get time consuming as you grow so I recommend using a fully integrated system. A CRM that is already integrated to client scheduling, employee, invoicing, payroll, and the back end databases will save time and money and reduce the chances of inaccurate entries. You add each contact only once—upon first interaction, and the system manages the contact through every stage of your sales and business system, whether it's a prospect, client, or employee.

Integrated CRM & Backend Systems:

August Systems Software
www.august-systems.com

eRSP, by Kaleida Systems
http://www.ersp.biz

Generations Home Care System
www.idb-sys.com

KanTime
www.kantime.com

One of the most comprehensive systems available is *eRSP, by Kaleida Systems* http://www.ersp.biz. eRSP is an Internet based employee scheduling application that automates many of your back end systems. This solution is designed specifically for home care service agencies, packaging contact management, employment records management, service inquiries, clients, assessments, follow-ups, time keeping, billing, payroll, scheduling, and more—all into the web-based interface. It's far easier to begin your business using this system than to try to migrate to the comprehensive systems later. If you've decided to use the cloud, this would be your all-in-one system.

The eRSP system has a relatively low setup fee and monthly fee to get you going for your first 1,000 billable hours. The monthly fees and setup charge are worth far more than the cost savings you'll receive. You can also reach them at 1-866-384-9265, ask for a free demo.

Set up Scheduling and Timekeeping System

A scheduling and timekeeping system helps you keep track of who is supposed to be where and when and for how long. You'll probably remember every detail of your first client's schedule. You may be able to do that with even 10 clients. But with all the activity that 10 clients will involve, you'll have little time to implement a schedule system outside of your own brain. Solution: set up your scheduling and timekeeping systems now.

Again, the more integrated your back end systems are jointly, the better. This includes your scheduling and time tracking system. Your scheduling system should be almost central to your timekeeping, invoicing, and payroll systems.

Many agencies still use paper timecards, But while carbonless, multi-page timecards worked well just a couple years ago, with today's technology, it makes no sense to even start with these. They are costly to print, distribute, collect, and enter into your computer systems for invoicing and payroll. They are also hard to verify accuracy. For instance, a care provider can easily "fudge" his or her time. A client with dementia may not realize the error and end up paying for service not received. Of course, most care providers are honest, but paper time cards often are filled out at the end of a shift or end of a week, by which time the care provider may inadvertently record the wrong arrival or departure times.

Technology called telephony can help prevent these mistakes. Using caller ID technology, Telephony requires the care provider to call from the client's home upon arrival and just before departure. It eliminates timesheets, verifies actual attendance of the care provider in real time, sends message alerts to management and supervisors when a care provider doesn't show up or is late, and streamlines both payroll and invoicing. And it's surprisingly inexpensive.

The telephony system is often separate yet integrated to scheduling and back office systems mentioned earlier. Several companies provide the telephony timekeeping and scheduling software systems, which can be used as back-office integration or individually:

ChronoTek—www.chronotek.net. Basic telephony and time scheduling.

MITC Software—www.mitcsoftware.com

Teletrak—www.teletrak.com. Provides the telephony and scheduling independently; however, it also integrates to eRSP and other back end systems.

Create Weekly Calendar of Activities

You're in business for yourself! The joy of that realization probably already surfaced when you had to decide when to get up this morning. But successful business owners know that just because they don't have a boss to tell them what to do, they still have to get out of bed. Successful business owners have learned how to use their time effectively and efficiently. The key to doing that is creating a schedule and following it consistently.

How much time do you plan to invest in your business each day and week? Whatever your answer, the time you do plan to work needs to be consistent, efficient, and effective. If you plan to put 20 hours per week in, that's just four hours per day without weekends, or three hours, seven days per week. Regardless of what works for you, you need to plan your schedule when you'll be focused on hiring, marketing, client relations, finance, operations, etc. Each of these areas needs your consistent attention.

One of the best ways to manage your time is to take your schedule by weeks and break the week down into areas. For example, you may choose to focus on recruiting employees on Tuesdays. This involves placing ads, reviewing applications, screening applicants, checking references, doing background checks, and making sure all the proper paperwork for each employee is in his or her file.

On Wednesdays, perhaps you choose to focus on marketing activities. This involves all the areas of getting your name out there—networking, placing ads, following up with referral sources, and getting a direct mail campaign put together.

Thursdays may include following up on client satisfaction—making follow-up calls and visits to make sure your staff are taking excellent care of your clients and doing their jobs right.

Every day you work, you will have interruptions. Some interruptions involve situations and activities that will require your immediate attention—but some are not so urgent. Having a consistent schedule of what you plan to do each week will help propel your success by forcing you to prioritize the issues that crop up. If you're not following a schedule - every issue will seem urgent; necessary tasks will fall by the wayside, yet you'll still seem busy. Avoiding necessary tasks doesn't make them go away; it only taxes your success.

Create Your Scripts

As you get out into the public, attend networking events and begin telling friends, family and people you meet about the business you've recently started – you will have to field questions. Before people start asking what you do, winging it is not the best strategy. Knowing what you're going to say is. You do this by preparing scripts in advance and practicing them so you make a solid first impression.

Creating scripts isn't difficult, although it takes some time to prepare, practice, and refine your script so that you don't sound like you're reading from a paper. Scripts should include the information you want to communicate to the inquiring individual, but you should still sound like yourself. After you follow the script enough times, it will begin to flow naturally. As your staff grows, they will be asked the same questions. The scripts provide them a consistent, systematic response to questions, reflecting the way you want your business to be presented.

The "Commercial" Script

The opportunities for you to present your "commercial" are everywhere, especially as you meet new people. Each meeting—whether at a networking event or during a chance encounter in an elevator—presents a short amount of time of opportunity for you to give them a concise, memorable "commercial."

What do you say?

30 Second Script:

"I'm with ABC Home Care Services, which provides in-home care services to seniors allowing them to stay in their own home—where they often prefer to be. We help those seniors by placing care providers in their homes to do daily tasks that you and I often take for granted—such as meal preparation, light housekeeping, laundry, errands, and transportation and medication reminders."

60 Seconds Script:

"I'm with ABC Home Care Services. Our company provides non-medical in-home care services to seniors, which allows them to stay in their own home. If given a choice between going to a senior living facility and staying at home, most prefer to stay at home. We help make this happen for them by placing care providers in their homes to perform daily tasks that you and I often take for granted, such as meal preparation, light housekeeping, laundry, errands, and transportation and medication reminders.

While our services help the seniors stay in their own homes, they also provide peace of mind to family members who aren't able to be there for their loved ones. Often the children or other family members don't live locally, have to work, or have their own children—these things prevent them from being able to help as much as they'd like."

Telephone Answering Script

Be consistent in your phone greeting. The caller may be a potential client, care provider applicant, or family member calling for the first time. You want to make a great first impression. Answer your phone with professionalism, positive energy, and a warm, cheerful greeting. Always smile while answering that call—callers can actually sense a smile through the phone.

Consider a script like:

"It's a wonderful day at ABC Home Care Services, how may I make it wonderful for you?"

Prospect Inquiry

When the caller indicates interest in knowing more about your services, you have a potential client. The goal of a prospect inquiry call is not to sell your services on the phone; it's an opportunity to learn about the prospect's needs, build rapport with the caller, qualify him or her as someone who may benefit from (and have the ability to pay for) your services, and schedule an assessment appointment.

Inquiry calls vary greatly. Some callers are calling simply to find out how much your services cost, and some are so burned out and frustrated that they could go on for hours explaining their situation. Still others don't know where to begin. Thus exact scripts won't always serve you very well. Following a set of objectives and questions is more helpful. We discuss the Prospect Inquiry in more detail in Chapter 9: Receive Inquiries.

Chapter 6 Review Task List

Upon completing Chapter 6, you should have:

❑ Created a filing system for paper and computer files.

❑ Created operations forms.

❑ Copies of operations form made and ready to use.

❑ Created prospect information packs (PIP).

❑ Purchased and set up a contact management system.

❑ Purchased and set up a scheduling and timekeeping system.

❑ Created a weekly calendar of consistent activities.

❑ Created your own commercial scripts.

❑ Practiced the commercial scripts.

Download editable forms, documents and more at
www.homecarehowto.com

CHAPTER 7

PREPARE FINANCIAL SYSTEMS

Create a Business Banking Relationship

Creating a solid relationship with your banker is essential. He or she will possibly be the one professional in your community who knows the most about your financial situation, so you'll need to trust the banker with that information. That trust should be earned. In turn, when and if you ever need to borrow money, your banker will be able to give you the best guidance possible in what you'll need to obtain the loan.

Good banks want to see your business grow and are willing to help you. Bank executives often know other businesses and many influential people within your community. They may be able to provide referrals to potential clients or businesses that could become great referral sources. And if you ever run into a snag with your banking, having a good relationship with them also makes it much easier to resolve it quickly.

Perhaps you already know your bank's VP or branch executive. If not, change that today! Ask your attorney or accountant to introduce you to any bankers they already know and trust. Check with your local chamber of commerce to find banks that are active in your community. Interview several. Select a bank or credit union that specializes in serving small businesses, embraces the in-home care services your business provides, recognizes opportunity in building a long term relationship with you, and provides account services that best fit your needs as a small business.

At each bank, ask to meet the vice president, branch manager, or branch executive. Ask the following questions:

❖ What types of businesses do they focus on?

❖ What is their specialty?

❖ Are they familiar with your industry, and do they serve other businesses in your industry?

❖ What types of accounts and products do they offer small businesses?

❖ What are the minimum balances required and fees associated with a small business accounts?

❖ Do they offer night deposits and online banking?

❖ What interest rates do they offer, both on credit cards and loans?

❖ Do they provide special loan programs for small businesses including SBA or other government-guaranteed or agency loans?

❖ How long have they been in their current position?

Some banks like to intimidate and throw their size and prestige around. Don't let them. Remember that you're in control of where you place your business account, and you are not obligated to pick the first one you visit.

Select the bank you want to do business with, and set up your account. Although initially you need only one account, soon you will need to set up a separate account for your payroll in order to simplify accounting. After your accounts are set up, make sure that you don't mix your business accounts with your personal bank accounts.

Set Up Accounting System

Today's software is extremely helpful for organizing accounting systems. Two main systems serve the small business industry—QuickBooks and Peachtree. QuickBooks leads the field and is probably the easiest to learn and most widely recommended. It also integrates into more of the scheduling, billing and contact management programs, including eRSP, which we discussed earlier.

Accountants and CPAs most commonly use QuickBooks, while some prefer Peachtree as their primary accounting software. Plan to invest between $160 to $200 for either software program and keep in mind that every two to three years you'll need to upgrade the software. For this small investment it pays for itself in just a couple months. For a bargain, go to www.ebay.com or Amazon for the same software at significant savings—just make sure it's an unused, unopened, register-able version. Intuit also has an online version that is only 9.95 per month—a great option if you're creating the business model operating within the cloud.

Both providers have their own merchant account provider solutions. A merchant account is a third-party vendor who handles the processing of credit card payments. Innovative Merchants, (QuickBooks' merchant provider) and Sage Payment Solutions (Peachtree's merchant provider) each allow you to accept Visa, MasterCard, Discover, and American Express payments at competitive pricing, and often much less expensive than competitors. One benefit from this relationship is that is you don't have to lease or purchase card swiping devices at additional fees (though you can if you wish), because everything is seamlessly integrated to the software.

Accounting Software Programs

Consider these two top accounting software programs:

Intuit's QuickBooks
http://quickbooks.intuit.com

Sage Peachtree
www.peachtree.com

Once you get your software, you'll first have to set up the chart of accounts. The software does this for you with the answers you give to a series of question it asks when you set up your software to a service business. Using the following chart of accounts example (based on the default accounts provided in QuickBooks), set yours up to include the following:

Sample Chart of Accounts 1

Bank Accounts	Bank
- Checking	Bank
- Savings	Bank
Accounts Receivable	Accounts Receivable
Employee Advances	Other Current Asset
Undeposited Funds	Other Current Asset
Accounts Payable	Accounts Payable
Refundable Deposits	Other Current Liability
Opening Bal Equity	Equity
Retained Earnings	Equity
CRT Visits	Income
Home Care Visits	Income
Interest/Fin Charges	Income
Other Services	Income
Advertising & Marketing	Expense
Amortization Expense	Expense
Automobile Expense	Expense
Bank Fees	Expense
- Maintenance Fee	Expense
- Merchant Account Fees	Expense
Contributions	Expense
Depreciation Expense	Expense
Dues and Subscriptions	Expense
Employee Background Check	Expense
Employee Gifts	Expense
Employee Reimbursements	Expense
Employee Training	Expense
Insurance	Expense
- Bonding	Expense
- Disability	Expense
- Liability	Expense
- Work Comp	Expense
Interest Expense	Expense
- Finance Charges	Expense
- Loan Interest	Expense
Janitorial Expense	Expense
Licenses and Permits	Expense
Miscellaneous	Expense
Outside Labor	Expense

Payroll Processing Fees	Expense
Payroll Taxes - Employer	Expense
Postage and Delivery	Expense
Printing and Reproduction	Expense
Professional Development	Expense
Professional Fees	Expense
- Accounting	Expense
- Legal	Expense
Recruiting	Expense
Rent/Lease	Expense
Repairs	Expense
- Equipment Repairs	Expense
Salaries & Wages	Expense
- Care Provider Wages	Expense
- Other	Expense
Supplies	Expense
- Care Provider Supplies	Expense
- Office Supplies	Expense
Taxes	Expense
- Federal	Expense
- Local	Expense
- Property	Expense
- State	Expense
Telephones & Internet	Expense
Telephony	Expense
Travel & Entertainment	Expense
Uniforms	Expense
Utilities	Expense
- Gas and Electric	Expense
- :Water	Expense

Set up Billing Invoices

QuickBooks and Peachtree create default invoices as you set up the system to a service industry. Using the default invoice as a guide, modify the provided invoice and statement templates. Adding your logo and slogan to them looks professional and is an important step in maintaining consistency with your company branding effort.

Billing Invoice Example

ABC Home Care Company

123 Main Street
Somewhere, AZ 88888

555-555-5555

Invoice

Date	Invoice #
6/1/2010	1

www.yourcompany.com

Bill To

Esther Capernacus
1234 Happy Valley Circle
Somewhere, AZ 88888

Terms	Due Date	Date
	6/1/2010	6/1/2010

Service Date	Service Description	Hours	Rate	Amount
5/20/2010	Home Care Services - Personal Care	1.25	20.00	25.00
	Out-of-state sale, exempt from sales tax		0.00%	0.00

Thank you for your business.

Total	**$25.00**

Hire an Accountant/CPA

Finding and hiring an accountant is as important as having a good banking relationship. Accountants do more than just crunch numbers. They assist with tax planning, business planning, networking, and your own personal tax planning— which very much involves your business. Their involvement in your planning stages is crucial as they can offer advice on everything from your bookkeeping systems (and bookkeeping services) to lease negotiations.

With all the automation that QuickBooks provides, you might be inclined to think you don't need a CPA or accountant. Don't be fooled! While the software keeps track of your accounting, your accountant uses this information to prepare quarterly financial reviews and statements that help with preparing the annual financial taxes. The accountant will help you understand all the financial information he or she prepares to help make adjustments in your business planning. Business planning also affects your personal tax returns and retirement planning; the accountant guides you with that as well.

To find a good accountant, look for the following:

What's his or her experience?
The accountant should specialize in small business and preferably be familiar with others in your industry.

CPA or Accountant?
CPAs are Certified Public Accountants and have taken tests to prove their proficiency in the profession. This designation isn't necessary unless a loan application or audit is being done. General accountants can also perform bookkeeping and tax preparation; someone who isn't CPA certified can still be a good accountant or financial advisor.

Are you comfortable with his or her personality?
You need to create a personal relationship with your accountant, so you want to be able to trust him or her and be able to communicate with him or her as a friend. Finding one who has common interests is very helpful.

How big is the firm that the accountant represents?
You probably don't need to hire a larger accounting firm.
Larger firms tend to do well with larger companies and don't
understand small business. Look for a smaller, more
personalized firm that focuses on helping small businesses.

Bookkeeping

Bookkeepers are different from accountants. Although many
accountants provide bookkeeping services, a bookkeeper's role
is rather straightforward: keeping the records (books) up to date
on where your money is coming in and going out, producing
monthly financial statements, and working with the accountant
on a quarterly and annual basis.

Each week you'll be receiving payments and needing to pay
vendors and employees. Compare the costs of training and
hiring a bookkeeper, doing the bookkeeping yourself, and having
the accountant or CPA do the bookkeeping for you. Bookkeeping
is a tedious process and you're in the business of focusing on
getting new clients, not tedious tasks.

Fortunately, bookkeepers are considerably less expensive than
an accountant and will save you time and effort. If possible,
outsource the bookkeeping from the beginning—this will free
your time to focus on the most important activities of marketing
and increasing your sales. Ask your accountant, attorney, and
chamber of commerce for recommendations of good
bookkeepers.

Set Up Payroll

An important piece of your financial team is your payroll
specialist.

Handling payroll is complex. It involves far more than just
adding up how many hours an employee works and multiplying
by their hourly rate. You must be compliant with federal, state,
and city taxes' Medicare; Social Security; workers'
compensation; unemployment insurance and more. Your

business is responsible for withholding correct amounts in accordance with current laws and knowing when to submit the payments to the various tax and insurance entities without incurring penalty.

It's complicated.

If you're planning to do the payroll yourself, strongly reconsider. Your time should be used in other areas, not on worrying about all the updates and requirements of payroll calculations. Your bookkeeper probably isn't current on the intricacies of payroll either. Second, if you or your bookkeeper do this task yourself, you're still on the hook if you make a mistake, and you'll need to spend many hours ensuring that you're current on the tax withholding laws, setting up systems to manage withholding amounts, and making payments to the respective government agencies at the proper time. Outsourcing these tasks to a payroll specialist company puts the liability on that company.

Payroll Providers

Consider the following national payroll service providers:

ADP
www.ADP.com

Paychex
http://smallbusiness.paychex.com/payroll

Peachtree Payroll
www.peachtree.com

QuickBooks Payroll
http://payroll.intuit.com

Third-party payroll providers such as QuickBooks or Peachtree have created their payroll services to integrate their payroll calculations into files that easily import to QuickBooks. The bookkeeper has only to import the file; the records are entered automatically.

Before signing on with QuickBooks or Peachtree payroll services, consider other providers (local and national), and compare pricing.

When comparing companies, ask:

❖ Do they guarantee the accuracy of their work?

- ❖ Do they run payroll reports monthly, quarterly, and annually?

- ❖ Do they provide digital files to upload to your accounting software?

- ❖ Do they handle all the tax withholding?

- ❖ Do they handle workers' compensation withholding?

- ❖ Do they complete and submit all tax filing forms and payments at the required times?

Establish Insurance Company Relationship

Part of your financial systems should include financial protection through insurance. The business of providing services in clients' homes via employees whom you can't monitor every minute entails liabilities. You need to offset your liabilities with insurance protection.

Establish a solid relationship with an insurance provider. Many insurance companies focus on specific areas, so you may need several insurance companies to provide each coverage. Consider an insurance broker to help you find these. Shop around for brokers to find the best rates.

Need Insurance Provider?

Looking for a first-rate insurance provider that focuses solely on insuring Home Care Agencies? Find them at: www.HomeCareHowTo.com.

The following are typically the types of insurance coverage you'll need. Consult with your insurance agent about the best policies and the necessary coverage for your business:

Comprehensive General Liability (CGL)

As long as you have employees, you'll have liability risk. CGL Is a broad form of liability insurance, covering claims for bodily injury and property damage and all general liability exposures on a blanket basis. It usually includes some form of contractual liability coverage.

Employee Bonding

Also known as Fidelity Bonding, this covers you and your clients for losses that are incurred as a result of dishonest and/or fraudulent acts of employees.

Extended Auto Coverage

Each of your care providers should carry his or her own auto insurance coverage, but this policy covers your own driving for business purposes and employees who use their car on your behalf.

Business Disability

This will protect you should you become disabled and not able to run the business.

Workers Compensation Insurance

This covers medical and rehabilitation costs and lost wages for employees injured at work. It's required by law in all states.

Health Care Insurance

Health insurance was once an optional benefit that employers could choose to provide. At the time of this writing, the health insurance reform bill is working through its stages of definition and requirements for small businesses.

Insurance is expensive, but as you grow, so does the possibility that someone in today's litigious society will come after you. As the saying goes, in lawsuits, no one wins—but if you're protected, you can still move forward and have a business. Without the proper insurance, you may lose not only your business but all your assets and many years of hard work.

Create Employee Pay Rates

What you pay your employees affects your bottom line— immediately! Establishing this rate will help you determine what rates to charge your clients.

The best way to determine what range to pay your staff is to find what the competition is paying care providers. Look at the Help Wanted (care providers) section in classified ads. You can also check www.Craigslist.com, your local newspaper's website, and so on. Respond to the ads as an interested applicant, and ask how much they pay. Keep in mind that the rates you learn about may be slightly skewed on the high end or low end. However it will provide a general range, which is what you're looking for.

Once you know the market's pay rates, calculate the "unseen" costs of your staff in addition to wages. These include costs such as insurances, federal and state taxes (different from an employee's withholding amounts, which will come out of the wage itself), unemployment, and any benefits that you offer.

The wage calculation table on the following page shows what costs would generally be in addition to the pay rate. Your state and even county may include additional taxes, so make sure you do your research to find out all the taxes you'll need to pay. Download an editable version at www.homecarehowto.com

Wage Calculator Table

	% Rate	$ Amount
Caregiver Hourly Wage		$9.00
State UIC	3.05%	$0.27
Social Security	6.20%	$0.56
Medicare	1.45%	$0.13
Workers Comp	4.00%	$0.36
(Optional) Liability & Bonding	1.00%	$0.09
(Optional) Admin Costs	22.00%	$1.98
(Optional) Transportation (est)	4%	$0.36
(Optional) Training	4.00%	$0.36
Total Additional Wage Burdens	45.70%	$4.11
Total Hourly Wage & Employer Burden		**$13.11**
Add Target Billable Hour Gross Margin	35.00%	$3.15
Minimum Hourly Billing Rate	80.70%	**$16.26**
Wage to Rate %	180.70%	

NOTE: Excluding Optional items from these calculation doesn't mean the costs won't be incurred. Your target rate will show as being lower, enabling a higher gross profit higher.

However, the costs will be incurred somewhere, reducing net profit in the end.

Notice when you divide the total hourly rate by the hourly rate of pay, you'll come up with 1.807, or 180.7 percent. Remember this in the coming section. Once you've determined the general range of pay for your employees, you can move on to the equally important step of creating service rates.

Create Service Rates

Establishing your rates is as important to your business' success as establishing pay rates. If you price your services too low, you're out of business before you begin—you just won't realize it until it's too late. If you set your rates too high, you may find it difficult to expand your client base as quickly as you project.

In the same way as you learned about how your competition is paying their staff, you want to know how much they are charging for their services. This knowledge will also give you a maximum rate that can pay your care providers.

Do you want to be the lowest cost provider? Do you want to provide excellent service for a fair price? Being the lowest price service can help you get yourself in the door; however, you'll find that offering the lowest price becomes a commodity game. You exchange low rates for high volume, however quality often suffers. Quality affects your reputation. A good reputation will shower you with referrals and increased business.

Here are calculation formulas to help you determine your rates:

A solid home care business plan target of 35 percent gross margin (and no less than 30 percent) is typically industry standard. Your gross margin is the fees you make after paying your care providers.

The equation for determining hourly rates to charge your clients is as follows:

Hourly Rate = Care provider Hourly Pay Rate x 180%
(Hourly Pay Rate) $9.00 x 185% = $16.20

Hourly Rate = $16.20

Remember that the wage costs coincide with your rates. When using the 180% of wage principle/formula, the 35% for your gross margin is factored in almost automatically.

In the above *Calculator*, the gross margin has already been added. The total cost of the hourly wage is added as is the percentage of those costs to the hourly rate. In the example, the hourly wage costs are an additional 45.7% over $9.00 per hour wage. Added to that is the gross margin of 35%, totaling 80.70%. Your rate becomes the wage plus wage costs plus margin desired, which works out very closely to the 180% principle.

Each state differs in taxes and workers compensation premiums. Make sure you use the exact tax and insurance rates to give you the best true hourly costs. This example shows workers comp costs at 4.0% of the wage per hour, but some states rates are lower and some higher. Generally, the 180% principle is a guiding tool. You should use this to help you determine your rates. A 30% margin to get your foot in the doors is not unreasonable. As you are proven and can show the high quality that commands higher rates, you may wish to bump up to a 35% gross margin. Aiming higher than that may price you out; aiming lower may cripple your operations capability and profitability.

After you have established your hourly rates, do the same process if you plan to provide additional services like:

❖ Live-in care

❖ 12- and 24-hour shifts

❖ Overnight care

❖ Serving two clients in the same visit
    (i.e., husband and wife)

❖ Mileage rates

Live-in care entails a care provider living in a client's home for one to four days at a time. The care provider isn't working that full amount of time, yet they're present in case something happens. Live-ins are typically structured as a per diem (per day) rate and offer discounted hourly rates given that the care provider isn't working the full 24-hour period.

Each state has differing laws about per diem pay scales, so research the state laws with the legal details (regular time, overtime, per diem rates, etc). As you contact your competition and learn about their rates, make sure you inquire about their live-in rates. Use the same formula and principles used for the hourly care to determine your live-in rates.

Twelve-hour and 24-hour rates are for clients who need continuous care. If the shift is an overnight one during which the care provider must remain awake, consider carefully before significantly discounting the rate.

Overnight care involves different levels (and is dictated by law in some states):

> **Level 1**—The care provider is able to sleep during the night, awakened no more than 3 times.
>
> **Level 2**—The care provider is able to sleep during the night, awakened more than 3 times.
>
> **Level 3**—The care provider must be awake throughout the night—no sleeping. This is typically the straight hourly non-discounted rate (and in some cases, overtime) because you're paying full labor rate in accordance with state and federal labor laws.

Consider the following as you set your service rates:

❖ Establishing a per visit charge which provides a caregiver to visit anywhere from 15 minutes to up to an hour and a half for a set flat rate. Setting up a service like this helps meet the growing need for short check up visits and gets your foot in the door to benefit from longer visits as they become necessary. This service requires hiring staff that is willing and able to accommodate short visits.

❖ Alternatively, set up a three or four-hour minimum visit as a general rule. This allows the care provider to complete all the tasks in the care plan while still making it financially worth his or her time to make the visit. If you assign care providers 1-2 hour visits to a client, whether once a week or five times per week, you may notice turnover in care providers willing to serve that client.

❖ Consider reducing minimum visit requirements to three hours when a client is committing to a schedule of three or more days per week.

❖ Charge an additional amount, another $1 to $4 per hour, when serving a couple. Caring for two people increases the demands on a care provider.

❖ Charge additional (from $1 to $5 per hour) for someone with memory loss such as dementia or Alzheimer's and require increased care levels.

❖ Charge additional (from $1 to $5 per hour) for those requiring considerable personal care — e.g., incontinence care, grooming and bathing, partial or full weight transfers, etc.

❖ Consider charging higher rates for clients seeking only weekend care. It can be more difficult to find employees willing to work only weekends. Competitively, you might find this difficult in some metro areas.

❖ Holiday visits should be charged at time and a half or more. Care providers expect holiday level pay, which is typically time and a half or double time.

❖ Establish a cancellation policy for clients who cancel service at the last minute. With the exception of emergencies, the full visit should be charged if not canceled 24 hours prior to the visit.

Establish Mileage Rates

Providing incidental transportation involves a care provider using his or her own vehicle. Charge the client a mileage rate if incidental transportation is provided. (It's easiest to use the current government mileage reimbursement rates; these fluctuate year to year.) Some agencies provide the first 10-15 miles per visit as part of the visit. If you do, be sure to communicate this expectation to the care provider prior to hiring.

Most states require that you pay the care provider mileage between the first client and the last client visits on the same day. This typically isn't chargeable to the client and is an expense to you, the employer.

Create Service List

Now that you've established your service rates, create a service rates document that explains the scope of each of your services along with the price. Include this document in your prospect information pack (PIP).

Your Logo Here

Reliable Home Care for Seniors

www.YourCompany.com (555) 555-5555

SERVICES & PRICING

Hourly Care Services

Our most popular service is designed for clients who benefit from assistance on a regularly scheduled basis each week. Care Plans and schedules are customized based on each individual's needs and Personal Assistants are available from 4 to 12 hours each day for one to seven days per week.

Companion Care Services From $XX per hour
Personal Care Services   From $XX per hour

Respite Care

Family Caregivers all deserve and should take time off from caring for their loved one. Using our Respite Care services will allow you to rejuvenate and refresh physically, mentally and emotionally, while a Personal Assistant takes care of your loved one.

Available 1 to 7 days per week, care is arranged only when you need it, on an intermittent basis. Whether it's once every few weeks or for a full vacation, our staff will give you the well deserved break you need.

Respite Companion Care From $XX per hour
Respite Personal Care   From $XX per hour

12-Hour and 24-Hour Care

When constant care is necessary, around the home or at bedside, daytime hours or around the clock, our trained Personal Assistants are at your beckoned call to assist anytime with Companion or Personal Care from 12 to 24 hours a day, 7 days a week.

12-Hour Care - from $XXX per visit

24/7 Monitoring

Using unobtrusive, assistive sensor technology, family has peace of mind with the ability to see everything is fine with mom or dad from any computer. Family is notified automatically if significant changes in routine are occurring, a fall in the shower, stove is left on and much more at fractions of the cost of 24/7 care.

Monitoring Services - from $XX per month*
*Equipment not included

Live-In Services*

A Personal Assistant "lives-in" your home for one to seven days per week.

Live-In services are ideal for individuals or couples who need care during the day, and the presence of assistance ready to serve in emergencies at night.

Available 1 to 7 days per week, care is arranged only when you need it. Whether it's once every few weeks or for a full vacation, our staff will give you the well deserved break you need.

Live In Care Services – Call for Rates

Details

*Live-In & Overnight Services requisites differ from hourly services offered. Please call for details.

+ Holiday services charged at 150% of normal rate.
+ Mileage invoiced at $.58/mile if care provider's vehicle is used.
+ Prices may vary depending on the level and variables of care needed

Prices subject to change

Serving Your County
Email : Help@YourCompany.com

Chapter 7 Review Task List

Upon completing Chapter 7, you should have:

❑ Met with and interviewed several banks.

❑ Formed a relationship with your new banker.

❑ Set up your business banking account(s).

❑ Purchased and set up your accounting system.

❑ Created your invoices and statements.

❑ Hired an accountant.

❑ Determined who will do the bookkeeping/hired a bookkeeper.

❑ Contacted and contracted with your payroll processor.

❑ Established a relationship with insurance company provider(s).

❑ Lined up insurance so that it is ready to go when you sign your first client.

❑ Established employee pay rates.

❑ Established service rates.

❑ Created mileage rates.

❑ Created a service list for marketing purposes.

Remember, you can download forms, spreadsheets, and other documents mentioned from the book's website www.homecarehowto.com.

CHAPTER 8

HIRING CARE PROVIDERS

As you launch your senior home care business, one of the most important steps for the success is implementing a system for hiring quality, well trained, dependable, compassionate, honest care providers.

To minimize the costs in your start-up phase, focus your hiring on part-time staff. When you're first getting started, you're more likely to be able to provide staff with only part-time hours.

It's best to hire experienced, trained, certified care providers. Someone who has been in the home care industry for at least two years understands the dynamics and logistics of providing care in the home. People who have cared for family members can also be a great asset to the company; however, there is a significant difference between providing care to family and to someone else.

Assuming you've done each of the steps listed so far, you're ready to move to the step that will shape the reputation of your business: finding care providers. Each step is important, but without excellent care providers, your agency's reputation will plunge. Your service hinges on whom you place in your clients' hands. Hiring excellent staff should be your top priority, but it will also be your most challenging task.

Finding help is easy; finding *good* help is *not* easy. In fact, it's a lot of work and once you've found great help, you want to keep them. Attention to this aspect will make you or break you, so pay close attention to the details of every employee you hire. They will represent your company, and you can't afford to have one person jeopardize the reputation and quality of your services.

The Care Provider Profile

When you place care providers into a home, you're entrusting them with your clients. They represent your company. Poor decisions they make for your client reflect less on them and more on you—and will reflect on you indefinitely.

Knowing what you're looking for makes your search easier. If you're just looking for warm bodies, you'll find loads of them. But if you're looking for a specific individual who meets your high standards, you must weed through the flood of applications to find the needles in a haystack. This requires more work, but the work will pay off.

Not all care providers are in the field because they feel called to it. The field is riddled with people who find themselves uneducated and decide that providing care to others would be an easy job. They're in the industry simply to have a job. These are not your best candidates. And some have been at it long enough (and jumped around enough) that they've become professional interviewers. They tell you what you want to hear.

The ideal care provider consists fits the following profile: *(There are exceptions to every rule, so while insisting on these may be tempting, keep an open mind until you meet the person and get a sense of his or her capabilities.)*

Experience
These applicants have at least one year of experience providing care. Be careful of those whose experience is limited to caring for family members. Providing care for clients is much different than caring for a loved one.

Background
An excellent care provider has a clean background. Of course, some excellent care providers have fallen into situations that may compromise their eligibility. But from a liability standpoint, it's in your best interest to proceed very carefully when presented with an applicant who has a felony on record. Your insurance company may not cover those who have previous convictions.

Age

More mature care providers seem to relate much better to seniors than do younger, energetic people fresh from college or high school. They also are wiser, more understanding, more patient, and have a better work ethic than the younger generation. You must not discriminate based on the applicant's age; still, you'll find that older folks seem to "get it" more than younger applicants. Seniors themselves are often naturally terrific care providers, especially for companion care services! So be cautious of hiring young applicants. While they may exude excitement and energy, they are often the same employees who leave you hanging with a phone call stating they aren't able to make it into work—10 minutes before they're supposed to be there.

Gender

Most care providers are women, but there are many male care providers who do a great job. Most clients first think of women when they consider care in their home, but occasionally clients (usually men) request male care providers.

Disposition

Hire only care providers who show that they are kind, patient, understanding, ethical, and compassionate.

Skills

An ideal care provider has good communication skills; speaks English and/or is fluent in another language of clients you wish to serve; is a good cook; is skilled at cleaning, laundry, and other household living activities; and has a good driving record and a valid drivers license with no more than one ticket.

Given these qualities, an ideal care provider profile begins to form:

❖ Mature—35 years or older.

❖ Experienced—One year or more (preferably at least two) of elder care experience.

- ❖ Compassionate, caring, patient, and understanding.

- ❖ Reliable, honest, and trustworthy.

- ❖ Highly ethical.

- ❖ Legally able to work in the USA.

- ❖ Wants to work part-time.

- ❖ No criminal history.

- ❖ Drug, alcohol, and smoke free.

- ❖ Able to drive and has a dependable vehicle.

- ❖ Clean and respectable appearance.

Prepare for Applicant Responses

Before you place ads or fliers or speak with those who may start referring applicants to you, set up an application process/system.

Envision a successful "Care providers Wanted" ad campaign. Many people are interested. Your phone rings constantly, and you feel as though you're making progress. You've spoken with at least 30 different applicants about how they can get your application, how to get it back to you, what you're looking for, how much you pay, and so on. It's exciting, at first. However after a few days of this, you may go nuts.

The solution: creating an applicant response system that answers all the questions once using either a telephone message or your website to provide the requirements and instructions in how to apply. Both methods prescreen qualified applicants while managing your time efficiently.

To set up an automated employment application system, you'll need either another phone number or a web based form that accepts applications via your website.

Phone Number Application System

To set up a phone number system, do the following:

1. Obtain another phone number. It can be a toll-free number if you're willing to pick up the costs for others calling the 800 line or a separate local phone number. The phone number does not have to be a live line—it can be a virtual number, which is a phone number that automatically goes to voicemail instead of ringing to a phone in your office.

2. Create a voice greeting on the phone number voicemail that explains the requirements and directions on how to apply.

Applicants who call this number hear a voicemail greeting that is 1-2 minutes long. The greeting includes details of what you're looking for, the qualifications required, the pay amounts, and instructions on how to apply.

Some agency owners prefer to have the applicants leave a name and number so they can call them back and get a "feel" for the applicant over the phone before they ever apply. Other owners prefer to have the applicant leave an address so they can mail the applications, and others have applicants pick up applications at their office. You could also direct them to your website to download a PDF or WORD Application to print out, complete, and send back to you. How you choose to have them apply is based on how much time you have or how many interruptions you're willing to deal with to find the right applicants.

Following is an example of what the greeting on your employment voice line may include. Modify it to fit your specifications:

Care Provider Employment Line Greeting

Thank you for your interest in employment with ABC Home Care Services. ABC Home Care Services provides non-medical in-home care services to seniors so they may remain in their own homes. We do this by assisting elderly individuals with activities of daily living, such as meal planning and preparation, laundry, light housekeeping, bathing, dressing, incidental transportation, errands, medication reminders, as well as companionship.

We are currently seeking all levels of care providers, including companions, past/present CNAs, and validly certified HHAs. Applicants should be warm, compassionate people with a heartfelt desire to work one on one with clients in their own home. The ideal candidates should be:

- Seeking part-time hours or live-in positions. While the hours are flexible, you must be willing to work at least three to four hours at a time. We will provide you with as many hours as possible through serving one or more clients.

- You must have at least one year of experience in providing care to the elderly.

- You must have your own vehicle and a valid driver's license with a relatively clean driving record.

- A CNA license or higher, current or expired, is a real plus, but not required.

We offer competitive pay beginning at $_____ per hour and up depending on your experience and level of care provided. If you meet these qualifications and would like to be considered as a potential member of our first-rate care provider team, obtain an application at _____ and return it to _____. Include your resume, and please write a brief paragraph about why you think you would be a great addition to our first-rate care provider team.
(You could, instead, ask them to leave their name and phone number if you prefer to call them back and talk with them first)
After receiving your application, we'll contact you for further details about our interview process. We receive a large volume of responses each day and will contact you as soon as possible upon checking our messages (daily, weekly).
Again, thank you for your interest in ABC Home Care Services, and we look forward to meeting you!

Once you've set up your phone system, be sure to integrate consistently checking your voicemails into your schedule. In the beginning you may want to check your messages each day; as you grow, it may be more manageable to check it once a week.

Web Site Application System

A web based employment application system is more streamlined than the phone application system. It is paperless, does not involve voicemail messages or returning phone calls, requires no postage stamps, and avoids interruptions by potential applicants who come to the office to pick up an application. Furthermore, running ads that put your website address on it allows you to include far more information about what you're looking for.

To set up the Web Application System:

1. Work with your website designer to create a web page that promotes careers/jobs with your company. The page should include details of the care provider position, the required qualifications, and the steps to take for the applicant to apply.

2. Create the Application Form. Use one or both of the following solutions for an applicant to apply via the web:

   a. Save and upload your employment application to your site in a PDF or Microsoft WORD format. Adobe provides a free PDF viewer in most Internet browsers. Microsoft WORD usually requires the applicant to have WORD installed on his or her computer, which limits potential applicants that don't.

   b. Have your web designer create a web based response form that includes all the questions you ask on the paper formatted employment application. A web based response form allows applicants to complete the employment application directly from your web page and submit it directly to you as an email with an attached resume.

3. Promote and include the URL of your employment application on all your care provider recruiting efforts.

Setting up the web based application form will require a bit more upfront time and costs than providing a downloadable application form. The convenience and time savings it will create in office administration is worth the investment. Be sure to discuss with your web designer all that's involved in setting up either solution.

Recruiting Care Providers

Plenty of care providers are available in today's job market. Your job is to find the needles in a haystack (i.e., the excellent providers).

So how do you have them come to you?

- ❖ Classified Advertising:

  - o Classified ads in newspapers.

  - o Website ads.

  - o Classified ad sites.

- ❖ Large job search.

- ❖ Workforce job center sites.

- ❖ Flyers.

- ❖ Networking:

  - o Community service organizations such as Lions Club, Rotary, and Kiwanis.

  - o COINs (Centers Of INfluence)—Leaders of your community and organizations that are well connected to others. They know those who need the help, or at least the people who would know.

  - o Church pastors and leaders.

❖ Senior Centers—Speak with the leaders in the center, and build relationships with them. Ask to place fliers in the senior center.

❖ Retirement complexes and communities often have a main social hall or activities center. Ask to post your flier and brochures there.

❖ Other care providers—Good care providers often know other good care providers. Ask your staff to help find other staff for you.

Placing Ads

One of the most successful ways of finding great care providers is placing ads. The least costly advertising is on the Internet, followed by local classified ads. Start placing ads on Internet classified sites, job search sites, and your local workforce development sites. Check with your local paper to find what day they run the biggest "Help Wanted" section. Place your print ads on that day.

Place your ads in the Senior/Elder Care or Health/Medical section of the classified section. Most care providers are searching under those headings.

Check the local community to find other websites or publications that offer employment classifieds. Below are some website suggestions to get you started:

Craigslist—www.craigslist.com. Posting to most metros on this site is free, though larger metropolis areas charge $25 to $75 per listing.

Kijiji — www.kijiji.com. All free classified ad postings.

Pennysaver—www.pennysaverusa.com. Relatively low cost; they publish on their website and in papers of the areas they serve.

Workforce Job Boards. Many state and county Workforce Development Agencies have job websites. These are government employment agencies and are eager to help you find qualified workers at low to no cost. Some agencies will allow you access to conference rooms and interview rooms for free or minimal cost. Check with your local workforce development/unemployment office for direction to their website.

The following job search sites are typically more expensive and may require numerous ads over time commitments for reduced rates; however, they may bring you more applicants than the other sites.

Career Builder—www.careerbuilder.com
HotJobs—http://hotjobs.yahoo.com

Print Publication Classified Ad Examples

The following are examples of successful newspaper ads. Costs are usually based on number of words, so the ads are shorter and more succinct:

CARE PROVIDERS

Seeking experienced, caring, reliable people to help seniors in their own home. Call 555-5555. www.yourcompany.com/jobs.htm

CNAs Wanted

Help the elderly in their own homes! Seeking experienced, certified CNAs for P/T and live-In positions. Visit www.yourcompany.com/jobs.htm

CARE PROVIDERS

Care for local elderly in their home. Valid CDL and car reqd. Exp pref. Hourly and live-ins. (555)555-5555 www.yourcompany.com/jobs.htm

HHAs Who CARE!

Help seniors and disabled at their home. Must have valid certificates! P/T or F/T 555-5555 or www.yourcompany.com/jobs.htm

Website Classified Ad Examples

Most Internet classified ad sites allow longer ads, allowing you to provide a detailed description of what you're looking for. Of course you'll provide the same detailed description on your website or in your automated phone message, but this is one more step in weeding out unqualified applicants before they apply.

The following pages include some example employment ads used in internet classifieds. Modify them to reflect your area and specific needs:

CAREGIVERS WANTED

ABC Home Care Services is looking for warm hearted individuals who enjoy serving seniors. We are a locally owned and licensed home care company providing **non-medical** services for seniors and others with special needs.

We are currently hiring care providers who can work days, weekends, overnights and 24 hour shifts in the Paradise Valley area.

The care services we provide to our clients include:

Companionship	Light Housekeeping
Meal Preparation	Bathing
Toileting Assistance	Shopping
Medication Reminders	Transportation
Mobility and Transfer Assistance	Organizing

We provide a positive, supportive work environment and are looking for flexible, honest, patient and reliable care providers with excellent oral and written communication skills. You must have a reliable and insured car, a good driving record, and a valid Texas Driver's License. We conduct background and reference checks on all employees. One year of experience is required, and a CNA certification is a huge plus, but not required. Compensation starts at $10.00 per hour.

To apply: Visit http://www.yourwebsite.com to complete an online application.

CNA or CHHA—Part Time

Highly respected home care company is looking for CNA (Certified Nursing Assistants) and/or Certified HHAs (Home Health Aides) to join our outstanding team of dedicated care providers. We provide non-medical care to seniors and disabled persons who want to remain in the comfort of their own homes.

WE ARE CURRENTLY FILLING SHIFTS FOR PART-TIME CARE PROVIDERS.

Care provider can be male or female. Duties include assistance with bathing/hair washing, meal preparation and feeding, medication reminders, escort to doctor appoints and medical treatments, assistance with home activities like light housekeeping, prepare grocery lists.

Candidates considered meet the following qualifications:

- Minimum of two years experience working with seniors
- Current CNA and or CHAA certification
- Experience with meal planning and preparation
- CPR certified
- 3 professional references
- Must be able to pass a criminal background check and drug screen
- Drivers license and social security card
- Current TB exam statement

We welcome qualified care providers who are seeking long term and rewarding relationships with our clients and our team. Please visit our website at www.yourcompany.com/jobs.htm, or call (555)555-5555 to apply.

Fliers

Another successful form of guerilla advertising and recruiting is using strategic placement of fliers. Fliers grab attention, are concise, and offer a way for the interested individual to respond. Post the fliers in public locations where lots of targeted ideal care provider traffic visit like:

- ❖ Senior centers

- ❖ Employment agencies and workforce development agencies

- ❖ Cafes that offer posting boards

- ❖ Churches

- ❖ Local college job centers

❖ Nursing schools

In the following example, notice the tear-offs at the bottom of the fliers with contact information. For higher and quicker visibility print the fliers on brightly colored attention grabbing paper.

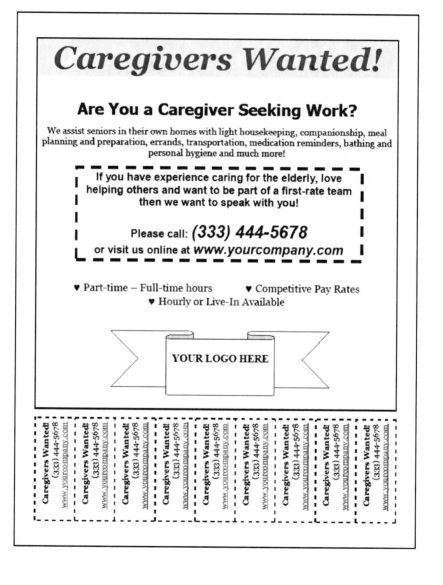

Networking

While networking within your community, connect with as many COINs (centers of influence) as you can. Let them know about your services and that you're looking for great help. Always have business cards and fliers with you to leave behind when someone asks how interested applicants can apply.

Join local associations and service organizations. Start with the local Chamber/Association of Commerce. Don't merely sign up—get involved in the events. Volunteer to assist on a committee or two that would benefit from your skills. Also attend meetings of service organizations such as Rotary International, Kiwanis, and Lions Club. Find one or two you are comfortable supporting, and get involved. Such organizations provide opportunities to give back to your community through volunteering your time, skills, and efforts while meeting like-minded business owners and community leaders.

As you become involved with these organizations, watch for opportunities to give speeches to the groups about your services. If you're uncomfortable speaking in public, consider joining a Toastmasters club to help you overcome that fear and improve your skills. www.toastmasters.org

Be careful not to over-commit your time to one or more organizations. At first you may have a lot of time to attend events and functions. Budget your time to include these events while being aware that as you grow, you'll still want to be active.

If you use each of these avenues, you will find plenty of interested applicants and qualified care providers. Find and hire the very best using your screening and interviewing process.

Employment Applications

If you've advertised and set up the applicant response system(s) properly, you'll weed out a lot of "bad fits" from those who are truly qualified.

Specific instructions on filling out an application helps prequalify serious applicants by revealing how well they follow instructions. If someone doesn't follow application instructions steps, how will they follow instructions and be responsible for your clients?

A truly qualified applicant should meet your list of requirements and fill out the application completely. Unanswered questions should raise questions to their attention to detail and reasons why a specific question wasn't answered. The following application is an example you can use. It's comprehensive and asks for a lot of details.

Replace this With
**Your Company
Logo Here.**

ABC Home Care Services We Help Seniors At Home
123 Somewhere St Anywhere, WA 98765
Phone: (333) 444-5678

Thank you for your interest in ABC Home Care Services.

ABC Home Care Services provides experienced, compassionate care to seniors and their families looking for reliable, trustworthy Care Providers. We receive many inquiries each day from people who are interested in qualifying to be on our first-rate care provider team.

To be considered as a team member with ABC, the following must be met:

1. Minimum 1+ years of experience providing care within the industry.
2. A dependable vehicle properly insured.
3. Valid *State* driver's license.
4. You must be trustworthy and dependable.

In addition to meeting the above criteria, the following documentation will be required:

1. Recent copy of your drivers license report (within last 6 months).
2. Copy of recent TB (Tuberculosis) screening (within last 6 months).
3. Background check completed.
4. Any certifications or degrees you may have earned.
5. Minimum of 3 verifiable professional references.

If you can meet all of the above, then completely read and fill out the enclosed questionnaire.

When you have completed the application, please fax, return by mail or drop off at our office listed above.

Thank you for your interest.

Sincerely,

ABC Home Care Services

130

Replace this With **Your Company Logo Here.**

Care Provider Application

By filling out this application and questionnaire, you are applying for employment at ABC Home Care Services. ABC Home Care Services is dedicated to a policy of non-discrimination of applicants on any basis including race, color, age, sex, religion, disability, medical condition, national origin, or marital status.

Your Full Name			Date	
Street Address		City	State	Zip
Home Phone	Cell Phone	Tax ID / SSN #	Do you smoke? ☐ yes ☐ no	
Date of Birth (Optional)	Ethnicity (Optional)	How did you hear about us:		

Alternate Contact

Name	Phone
Address	Relationship

Are you currently employed / provide Care to others? If Yes, Explain. ☐ yes ☐ no	Explain:

Have you ever been convicted of a misdemeanor/felony? If Yes, provide details

☐ yes ☐ no   Details:

Transportation:
Most clients require transportation, often using the Care Provider's vehicle:

Do you have dependable transportation? ☐ yes ☐ no		Make and model car	
License plate #	Driver license #		Auto insurance policy #
Insurance company	Insurance agent name		Insurance agent phone

Availability

Appx. hours per week available:	Days/Times you are available	Days & times not available	Can you be called at the last minute in case of emergency? ☐ yes ☐ no
Select the areas that you will accept work:			

☐City 1 ☐City 2 ☐City 3 ☐City 4 ☐City 5

1/07   Employment_Application_HomeCareHowTo1

131

What Education Qualifies You To Work As a Care Provider?

High school	City/State	Dates
College	City/State	Dates
Other	City/State	Dates

Degrees/certificates – All Degrees / Certificates must be presented copy. All will be verified with provider/issuer.

Special skills or courses – Any skills that assist in making you qualified as a professional Care Provider.

What is Your Past Experience?

Discuss any training or experience working with the elderly. How are you trained and/or experienced in working with the elderly?

What do YOU do that shows and proves you're Reliable, Trustworthy and Honest?

What would you like least about working with the elderly?

Skills

Please indicate which of the following skills you are prepared to provide if referred to seniors / families:

Companion Care & Safety	☐ yes	☐ no	Medication reminders	☐ yes	☐ no	Oral Care	☐ yes	☐ no
Alzheimer's	☐ yes	☐ no	Transportation	☐ yes	☐ no	Shaving Assistance	☐ yes	☐ no
Dementia	☐ yes	☐ no	Bathing (Reg., bed, sponge)	☐ yes	☐ no	Assist w / P.T. Exercises	☐ yes	☐ no
Meal Prep / Clean Up	☐ yes	☐ no	Dressing/ Grooming	☐ yes	☐ no	Assist w/ Prosthesis	☐ yes	☐ no
Feeding	☐ yes	☐ no	Incontinence	☐ yes	☐ no	Hospice	☐ yes	☐ no
Light Housekeeping	☐ yes	☐ no	Ambulation	☐ yes	☐ no	Willing to Work w/Pets	☐ yes	☐ no
Laundry	☐ yes	☐ no	Transfer assist	☐ yes	☐ no	Speak fluent English	☐ yes	☐ no

1/07 Employment_Application_HomeCareHowTo – Page 3 of 5

132

Work History

Please provide at least five years of recent, verifiable work history followed by verifiable references.

Company	From	To

Job title	Reason left

Duties

Supervisor	Phone

Company	From	To

Job title	Reason left

Duties

Supervisor	Phone

Company	From	To

Job title	Reason left

Duties

Supervisor	Phone

Why Do You Feel You Would Be An Excellent Addition to ABC Home Care Services Team?

Business | Professional References

Name	Address	Relationship/Years Known	Local Phone #
Name	Address	Relationship/Years Known	Local Phone #
Name	Address	Relationship/Years Known	Local Phone #

133

Character & Personal References

Name	Address	Relationship/Years Known	Local Phone #
Name	Address	Relationship/Years Known	Local Phone #
Name	Address	Relationship/Years Known	Local Phone #

CERTIFICATION AND RELEASE: I certify that I have read and understand the general requirements of ABC Home Care Services on page one of this form and that the answers given by me to the foregoing questions and the statements made by me are complete and true to the best of my knowledge and belief. I completely understand that I am submitting this Application for Employment and that any false information, omissions, or misrepresentation of facts called for in this application may result in rejection of my application and/or employment if hired. I authorize the company and/or its agents, including consumer reporting bureaus, to verify any information including, but not limited to, work, criminal and credit history and motor vehicle driving records. I authorize all persons, schools, companies, and law enforcement authorities to release any information concerning my background and hereby release any said persons, schools, companies, and law enforcement authorities from any liability for any damage whatsoever for issuing this information.

Signature	Date

For Office Use Only – Interviewer Comments | Reference Check Results | Notes

134

Reviewing Applications

Your first line of screening is weeding out people who don't qualify before they apply. Reviewing the applications is the second line of filtering out mediocre care providers.

As you review each application, look for the following:

Legibility and neatness. If you can't read the writing, it's going to be difficult to read the documentation logs that are filled out at each client visit. Spelling can be an issue too. While some spelling errors can be overlooked, the writing shouldn't read like a foreign language.

Completeness. Is the application entirely filled out? Has each question been answered completely? How thoughtfully has it been answered? Did the applicant leave blanks? If so, the applicant isn't detail oriented and has issues with not completing tasks. These shortcomings will show up in service to clients as well.

Resume. Resumes also show how much or little thought is being put into the effort. If you require a resume as part of your application process and one isn't attached, you probably don't want a worker who doesn't follow through on details.

Job History. Is job history sporadic? Has the applicant worked many different places? How long was he or she at each job? An applicant who jumps from job to job will jump from your job as well.

Drivers License. Does the applicant drive and have a vehicle? Trying to work with care providers who can't drive or don't have a car is difficult in most areas. Disqualify these applicants to save yourself time and headaches.

References. Are business and personal references provided? Personal references alone don't cut it. You want as many references as possible. If an applicant provides a limited few, there's a good reason. Most excellent workers know at least three previous employers, co-workers, and personal non-friends they can list quickly.

Your Gut. What does your gut feeling say about the person from what is presented to you on paper? Does it look like the applicant has put their best ability to truly shine?

After reviewing the application, ask yourself, Do I want to invest time to learn more about this person and meet him or her? If you do, then move to the next step and set up an Interview.

Interviewing

The interview is an integral part of putting together a first-rate team of care providers. An application can tell you a lot about an applicant; however, meeting and interviewing an applicant provides much more insight into them while communicating to them how serious you are about conducting a first-rate business. If you rush through the interview process, you will eventually (if not immediately) encounter problems with your staff. But when you put careful thought and attention to those you hire, managing higher quality staff is much easier because applicants recognize that your company places high expectations on their performance.

Set up a consistent interview schedule each week. If you operate your business from your home, conduct interviews in a coffee shop, library, or government workforce development/employment center. (In fact, conduct all business with applicants or employees in public places for safety and security.)

Interviewing is as much an art as a skill. It may seem daunting at first; however, it's not difficult, and you'll quickly get the hang of it. As you conduct each interview, ask yourself if you would entrust your parents, family, or friends into this person's care. Follow your instincts.

A few key points to remember before and while interviewing:

> ❖ A person's history is indicative of future performance. Look for previous employment or experience involving caregiving.

❖ Don't hire someone simply because you like his or her personality. Having a great personality doesn't make someone a great care provider. Ask how well the person will do the job.

❖ Ask open ended questions. Questions that require a yes or no answer won't tell you very much about the candidate. You want applicants to talk about themselves to help give you a better picture of who they are and their capabilities.

❖ Never make the decision to hire someone on the spot. Take some time after the interview to complete the interview assessment form. Don't rush a hiring decision.

Interview Preparation

Prepare for each interview by reviewing the applicant's application. Make notes on the interview questionnaire and highlight areas on the application that contain questionable answers.

❖ Is the application filled out completely?

❖ Has the applicant included references for both personal and business without duplicating the names or listing family members?

❖ Did the applicant include his or her driver's license and insurance information so that you can verify the information given?

❖ Does the work history make sense with the dates listed? Are there gaps? Why? Are the dates vague or concise?

The Interview

When you first meet candidates, smile and greet them warmly. Understand that they may be nervous and uncomfortable in interview situations. Break the ice with pleasant small talk, and put them at ease so that you can meet the goal of the interview: finding out if the applicant has the qualifications, characteristics, and skills of an excellent care provider and employee.

The interview is as much about asking questions to learn about the candidate's qualifications as it is about reading between the lines to find answers to the unasked questions.

Does the candidate:

❖ Show signs of compassion, care, and sincere desire to help others?

❖ Use common sense?

❖ Display respect, patience, and courtesy?

❖ Show signs of being a good fit on your team of excellent care providers?

❖ Show integrity?

❖ Have the aptitude to provide excellent care?

❖ Have a willingness to learn and be trained?

❖ Follow through in completion of tasks?

❖ Follow directions well with attention to detail?

Begin your interview with some open ended questions:

❖ "Tell me about yourself."

❖ "What kind of work have you done in the past?"

❖ "What inspired you to want to work as a care provider and apply for work here?"

❖ "What was your favorite/least favorite job you've done in the past and why?"

After each question, look directly at the candidate, and be silent. Let the candidate speak, don't interrupt, and give a moment of pause after the response before asking another question.

The form on the following page is provided as an example of questions to ask during each interview.

Applicant Interview Questions

Applicant Name: _____   Date: _____

Interviewer: _____   Time: _____

Interview #:   (1)   (2)   (3)   Application Turned In? (YES) (NO)

Intro: *(Background of the individual)*

Why are you interested in Caregiving? _____

What do you like most about elderly? _____

What are some of your hobbies and interests? _____

How did you hear about the position? Who referred you? _____

Experience
_____Year(s) of Experience

Tell me about your experience with the elderly/ providing

care?_____
_____

Tell me about your past employment / prior work experience (within this field)

_____

Tell me about 2 experiences you've had in caring with/for elderly people.

_____
_____

Are you currently working?_____

What was your last job?_____

Why did you

leave?_____

Education
What is your educational background? _____

What professional licenses/ certifications have you achieved? Valid or expired *(ie CNA, HHA, RN, CPR, First-Aide)*

License:_____ Expires _____	CNA HHA RN LVN	
License:_____ Expires _____	CPR 1ˢᵗAide Companion Homemaker	
License:_____ Expires _____		

Notes:
_____
_____
_____

Background Checks

Are you aware that we perform extensive background checks on every employee we hire going back 10 years for felonies & misdemeanors?

We care for people who are vulnerable, and, have to make very sure that the caregivers we hire are people who do not present any risk to our clients in any way. Because of that, I need to ask you some questions that are a little touchy, but very important. IF you answer yes to any of these, it doesn't disqualify you from the job, it means we need to discuss it further. Honesty is key since we do thorough checks of our own.

1) Have you ever been convicted of a felony?   Yes | No
   IF YES, Explain: _____

2) Have you ever faught with or had problems with drugs or alcohol abuse?   Yes | No
   If YES, Explain: _____

3) Do you smoke?   Yes | No
   If YES, are you able to go several hours w/o a cig? _____

4) Have you ever contracted a communcable disease for which you may now be a
   carrier like Tuberculosis, malaria or other disease?   Yes | No
   Explain: _____

5) Do you have any physical problems that would prevent you from assisting a client in any
   way?   Yes | No

Job Description

In your opinion, what do you think providing excellent care and/or being an excellent caregiver is?_____
_____
_____

Can you explain what you think your job description/responsibilities/duties might include if we employed you?
_____
_____

Describe what "EXCELLENCE" MEANS: _____

Do you believe your life exudes EXCELLENCE?_____

Describe how _____

What do you know about our Company? _____

Why do you want to work for our company? _____

Why should we hire YOU? _____

Are you reliable? Dependable? How could you prove that?_____

Are you willing to prove yourself over a 45-90 day period?_____

What do you think would be the most challenging part of a caregiver position?_____

What do you like most and least about caregiving? _____

Notes:
_____
_____
_____

-- 2 --

141

Service Activities employees perform each day:

Service Area
How far are you willing to travel for assignment?

_____

_____

_____

_____

_____

Incidental Transportation
We provide some clients with shopping ,errands, and incidental transportation.

Valid Drivers License?	Yes		No
Do you have your own car?	Yes		No
Fully insured?	Yes		No
Do you have a copy of current policy?	Yes		No

What's your experience in providing transportation/errands?
Yes | No

What kind of car do you drive? (Year, Make & Model)

_____

Housekeeping & Laundry
We provide light housekeeping services to our clients:

What are your laundering methods? _____

_____

If you had a client and you noticed things were not very

clean, how would you handle the situation?_____

_____

What kind of housework do you consider reasonable within a Home Care setting? _____

_____

_____

Prepare Meals
In your opinion, what's your level of cooking skills (on a scale of 1-10)?

Cooking meals for other people?   Yes | No

Do you consider yourself good at it?   Yes | No

Cooking meals for people with special dietary needs?
Yes | No

What type of food do you typically make? *(ethnic, style, etc)*

_____

What kind of dinner would you make for an elderly person on a low to no sodium diet? A Diabetic client?

_____

_____

Medication Reminders

How would you define "medical" VS "non-medical" care?

_____

_____

Tell me about your experience with those with medical challenges that can be debilitating?

_____

How would you handle a medical emergency?

_____

_____

Provide other assistance where needed
Some clients also need assistance with things such as:
Please tell me about your experience with:

1.	Monitoring bathing & safety	Yes		No
2.	Sponge Bath/bathing	Yes		No
3.	Moving of items/furniture	Yes		No
4.	Overnight care	Yes		No
5.	Continence Care	Yes		No
6.	Organizing the home	Yes		No
7.	Lifting of tools/ wheelchairs,etc.	Yes		No

What tasks mentioned would you have most trouble with?

_____

_____

NOTES: _____

_____

- 3 -

142

Dealing with Difficult People

Occassionally, clients struggle with issues like Alzheimers disease or dementia which causes them to be difficult to deal with.

Describe working with someone who is difficult to deal with?
_____

Describe your most difficult patient:
_____

How did you address the situation?
_____

What made the person difficult
_____

How did you handle the situation?
_____

What would you do if a client became difficult?
_____

How do you handle yourself in a situation like this?
_____

Hours Available To Work

❑	*Sat*	*AM*	*PM*
❑	*Sun*	*AM*	*PM*
❑	*Mon*	*AM*	*PM*
❑	*Tues*	*AM*	*PM*
❑	*Wed*	*AM*	*PM*
❑	*Thu*	*AM*	*PM*
❑	*Fri*	*AM*	*PM*

Live-Ins, Emergencies & On-Call

Are you willing to do 24 Hr Live-Ins?   Yes | No
How many consecutive days?
     1day | 2days | 3 day | 5+ days

Avail for emergencies or 'on-call'?   Yes | No

Placement & Wages

If hired, there may be a period of time before we fill your schedule.   Yes | No
Are you able to withstand this financially as we fill your schedule?   Yes | No
Do you know what we pay our caregivers?
                                   Yes | No
What are your thoughts about the compensation?
_____

Final Word

Is there anything else you feel I should know or what final thought would you like to leave me with?
_____
_____
_____

We've got a few other applicants to interview. I will evaluate all we have talked about, conduct reference and background checks and we'll call you if a second interview is needed. Thank you for coming in!

NOTES:
_____
_____
_____
_____
_____
_____
_____
_____

Post Interview Assessment

Immediately following the interview, assess the candidate using an interview assessment form (example provided at the end of this section). Complete it while the interview is still fresh. Don't wait several hours, especially if you are interviewing several candidates in a row.

While completing the interview assessment, think about the interview as a whole, and, using the numerical scoring system, rate the interviewed applicant on each area.

Ask yourself these questions as you complete the assessment:

- ❖ What was your overall impression of the candidate?

- ❖ Would you place your parents, family, or friends into the care of this candidate?

- ❖ Does the candidate appear to be caring, compassionate, and ethical?

- ❖ Was the candidate on time and reflect dependability?

- ❖ How was the candidate dressed?

- ❖ Does the candidate understand the service tasks that will be expected?

- ❖ Does it seem like the candidate will perform the job well?

- ❖ Will the candidate be an excellent representative of your company?

Interview Assessment Form

Applicant Name: _____   Interviewer: _____   Date: _____

1 = Unsatisfactory   2= Satisfactory   3= Average   4= Above Average   5=Exceptional

Job Related Requirement		Rating 1 to 5	Rating Comments
1	Appearance/Grooming		
2	Dependable/Timeliness		
3	Enthusiasm/Initiative		
4	Verbal Communication/Language		
5	Interpersonal Skills/Team Player		
6	Maturity		
7	Compassion, Caring & Patient		
8	Educational Background		
9	Schedule Availability/Flexibility		
10	Will Cover Full Service Area		
11	Clean Criminal Record		
12	Work Experience/History		
13	Dementia Experience		
14	Cooking & Homemaking		
15	Personal Care & Toileting		
	Add Total Ratings:		
	FINAL SCORE:		(Divide Total Ratings by 15)

Interviewer Comments:

_____

_____

_____

_____

_____

_____

Recommended Action:

_____Setup 2nd/ 3rd Interview   _____ Other:_____

_____Retain App for future consideration   _____ Do Not Hire:

_____Hire Applicant   Reason for Not Hiring:

Reason for Hiring:_____   _____

_____   _____

©2010 Home Care How To

Reference Checks

If the candidate proves to measure up to the assessment requirements, then perform personal and business reference checks.

Using the following Reference Check Forms for Previous Employment and Personal checks, call the past employers to verify the candidate's information and ask about the candidate's history with that employer. Before you complete your call ask if they would ever re-hire the person

After completing your reference checks, decide if you'll hire the candidate or not.

REFERENCE CHECK FORM

Applicant Name: _____

Business / Previous Employment

Company Contacted: _____   Reference Contacted: _____

Dates of Employment: __/__/__ to __/__/__   Would you rehire this individual?   YES | NO

Attendance History : _____   What the individual's Strengths/ Weaknesses?

Reason for leaving: _____   _____

_____   _____

Other_____   Other _____

*Reference Contacted By:*_____   *Date Contacted: __/__/__*

Company Contacted: _____   Reference Contacted: _____

Dates of Employment: __/__/__ to __/__/__   Would you rehire this individual?   YES | NO

Attendance History : _____   What the individual's Strengths/ Weaknesses?

Reason for leaving: _____   _____

_____   _____

Other_____   Other _____

*Reference Contacted By:*_____   *Date Contacted: __/__/__*

Company Contacted: _____   Reference Contacted: _____

Dates of Employment: __/__/__ to __/__/__   Would you rehire this individual?   YES | NO

Attendance History : _____   What the individual's Strengths/ Weaknesses?

Reason for leaving: _____   _____

_____   _____

Other_____   Other _____

*Reference Contacted By:*_____   *Date Contacted: __/__/__*

REFERENCE CHECK FORM

Applicant Name: _____

Personal References

Reference Name: _____ References Phone #: _____

Reference Address: _____

How do you know the Applicant? _____ What do you feel their Strengths/ Weaknesses are?
_____ _____

How long have you known the Applicant? _____ _____
_____ _____

How well does he/she get along with others? Other Comments:
_____ _____
_____ _____
_____ _____

How do you think the Applicant would do as a Care Provider? _____

Reference Contacted By: _____ Date Contacted: ___ / ___ / ___

Reference Name: _____ References Phone #: _____

Reference Address: _____

How do you know the Applicant? _____ What do you feel their Strengths/ Weaknesses are?
_____ _____

How long have you known the Applicant? _____ _____
_____ _____

How well does he/she get along with others? Other Comments:
_____ _____
_____ _____
_____ _____

How do you think the Applicant would do as a Care Provider? _____

Reference Contacted By: _____ Date Contacted: ___ / ___ / ___

Hiring Administration

Once you've hired the employee and collected all of the hiring documents, create the employee file and add the new employee to your payroll processing system. Use the employee file checklist that follows to ensure that you have the necessary documents on file; this also keeps your employee files consistent.

Employee File Checklist

EMPLOYEE NAME:

INTERVIEW DATE: /   /   DATE OF HIRE: /   /

TRAINING MANUAL ISSUED DATE: /   /   ORIENTATION DATE: /   /

EMPLOYEE ENTERED TO SYSTEM DATE: /   /

PAY RATE(S): Hourly $_____ Live In $_____ Per Day   DIRECT DEPOSIT: YES | NO

REQUIRED DOCUMENTS
Each of the following documents must be included the employee file:

- ☐ Employee Application
- ☐ Employee Interview(s)
- ☐ Interview Assessment(s)
- ☐ Reference Checks

- ☐ Background Check from State
- ☐ Background Check from 3rd Party Provider
- ☐ I-9 Completed
- ☐ W-4 Completed

- ☐ Copy of Social Security Card
- ☐ Copy of Drivers License
- ☐ Copy of DMV Record
- ☐ Copy of current auto insurance card
  Exp. date: _____

- ☐ Signed Employment Agreement
- ☐ Signed Confidentiality/Non-disclosure Agreement
- ☐ Signed Job Description
- ☐ Signed Policies & Procedures

- ☐ Copy of TB Test Results (last 12 months)
- ☐ Copy of First Aid Certificate
  Exp. date: _____
- ☐ Copy of CPR Certificate
  Exp. date: _____
- ☐ Copy of HHA Certificate
  Exp. date: _____
- ☐ Copy of CNA Certificate
  Exp. date: _____

- ☐ Copy of Other Certification:
  Type: _____
  Exp. date: _____
- ☐ Copy of Other Certification:
  Type: _____
  Exp. date: _____
- ☐ Copy of Other Certification:
  Type: _____
  Exp. date: _____

Assuming that you've completed all the tasks in Chapter 6: Create Your Files System, you should be seeing how all your efforts are paying off and coming together.

Care Provider Training

Your new employees are representing you. They will be providing (or not providing) the excellent services around which you want to build a reputation. If you fail to train your employees according to your expectations, they will do their job the way THEY think they should. They're almost certain to have a different perspective than yours if you don't give them proper direction through consistent and effective training.

Training is ongoing; it's not a one-time event. Plan to train your employees at several different intervals.

New Hire Orientation and Training

When you've decided to hire a new employee, set an appointment for the new hire orientation training. The purpose of this appointment is to get the necessary documents signed as well as to orient and train the employee. When you explain the importance of the Orientation and Training appointments, pay special attention to the employee's response. If he or she hesitates or protests, reconsider your decision to hire this person. You want only an attitude of excellence in your organization.

Don't rush the orientation and training—it should take at least three hours. If it will take longer than four hours, consider splitting the training into two appointments so that all of the information can be absorbed.

Schedule the training appointment with several new care providers at once to make the most efficient use of your time. Set specific dates through each month for orientation and have all new staff attend that date.

The new hire orientation training should include in detail:

- ❖ Completing and signing the new hire employee documents.

- ❖ Collecting all the necessary employee documents.

- ❖ Discussing the company's history, mission, vision, and values and the importance of adhering to these.

- ❖ Discussing company policies and procedures.

- ❖ Reviewing the employee handbook,

- ❖ Discussing the importance of employees' role to the company—how their performance shapes the company's reputation and success,

- ❖ Emphasizing the importance of the care providers' role in the company and how their performance influences the company's reputation and success.

Use this orientation time to get to know the employees. If at any point during this process the care provider indicates through words or actions that they are uncomfortable with what you're covering, it's a sign that they won't follow your guidelines of excellence. Explore and question these hesitations. This person may not be a good representative of your company after all.

New Client Orientation

Each client will have specific instructions that are covered in the his or her care plan. It's essential for the care provider to be very familiar with the care plan for each client that he or she will care for. Review these plans with the care providers in detail. Care plans will be covered in detail in Chapter 9: The Care Plan.

Ongoing Skills Training

Encourage ongoing education and self-improvement of the care providers in every way possible. You must separate your company from the competition by providing well educated and trained staff.

Set up these training sessions of 1 to 3 hours events on a monthly basis. Require all staff to attend these training sessions.

The monthly training sessions accomplish a few things. They help you gauge the staff's understanding and skills while building your team's camaraderie and loyalty to your company. They allow care providers to share their experiences, build friendships, and feel more connected with the company. Many of the staff ordinarily see only their clients and you; these sessions will help them feel like an important piece in a bigger organization.

Suggestions for ongoing training sessions:

❖ Organize them yourself and invite members of the community that specialize in various areas of specialty (i.e., dementia, Alzheimer's, CPR, first aid, fire safety, home safety, EMTs) to speak to your employees.

❖ If yours is a home based office, research venues in your community that are willing to let you use their meeting rooms, conference rooms, etc. Check out the library, senior centers, and service organizations.

❖ Consider opening the training sessions up to not only your care providers but also to the general public. This is a good way to build relationships and give back to your community while sharing helpful information.

❖ Plan some of the sessions (every three to six months) around a gratitude dinner or company function for your staff to thank them for their work.

❖ Some care providers won't be able attend every session, as they may be serving a client at the time you've scheduled the sessions. Consider scheduling two different training times if possible or rotate the training schedule.

Managing Employees

Just as you create ongoing training for your employees, you should set up an ongoing training system for yourself and your management staff. Many books and classes are available to help with varying management styles. Finding the books and classes that best fit your vision is up to you. Consider some of the employee management books to get you started. If management isn't actively improving their own skills with ongoing training, employees will probably follow suit.

Reading books and taking classes will take time. The following key points will help manage employees from the starting gate.

Communicating the Basics

Managing your staff effectively begins with communication—the training discussed earlier. Thorough training from the beginning gets you off to a great start but requires ongoing reiteration, motivation, and enthusiasm.

Employee Management Books:

Employee Training and Development by Raymond Noe

How to Hire, Train and Keep the Best Employees for Your Small Business by Dianna Podmoroff

Make It Glow: How to Build a Company Reputation for Human Goodness, Flawless Execution, and Being Best-in-Class by Tom Decotiis

Employees want to know that they are a part of an organization that has structure, vision, and a clear direction. If they sense they are working for an organization that has loose management, standards, and processes, they'll feel lost and perform in a way that can destroy your organization. Consistently and clearly communicate the company's vision, mission, and values, and align your decisions, goals, and focus accordingly. It will be obvious to your staff if they are not in line.

You'll have ongoing opportunities to do this, starting with the new hire and training and continuing at your monthly training meetings, periodic employee reviews, supervisory visits to client homes, company events, staff meetings, employee appreciation events, and other events.

Client Input

One of the clearest ways of knowing whether your employees are fulfilling your expectations for them is through client input. Your clients provide your paycheck; thus they are your boss.

Obtaining client input requires ongoing communication. Speak regularly with the clients, their families, and others

Customer Survey Service Companies

Consider outsourcing your surveys to one of the following:

Pinnacle Quality Insight (specializes in the health care industry)
www.pinnacleqi.com

Question Pro (Web based and offers free survey templates)
www.questionpro.com

Sinclair Customer Metrics—
www.sinclaircustomermetrics.com

involved in their care. Conduct supervisory visits, and ask about the quality of services they receive.

Consider sending clients surveys or comment forms on a quarterly or semi-annual basis at minimum. You may begin by doing this on a quarterly basis and, as your client base grows, outsource the task to a company that specializes in customer satisfaction survey services. The company will aggregate the feedback they receive into measurable progress reports. Many clients are more inclined to honestly express their opinions about your services if a third party is asking the questions.

Supervisory Visits

Conducting supervisory visits to clients' homes can help you ensure that employees are doing what they are supposed to. Some visits should be scheduled and some unscheduled. Visit new care providers more frequently so that you can not only make necessary corrections but positively reinforce good work. When a care provider is first assigned to a client, visit in the first and second week and, depending on performance, visits in the third and fourth week also. After that, depending on what you see, conduct a monthly visit at minimum.

During these supervisory visits you'll be observing and listening for feedback from both the client and the care provider. You'll be advising your employee of necessary changes and praising him or her for work well done. Holding employees accountable and requiring attention to detail is essential—especially in the early few weeks of the new assignment. As employees prove themselves and your trust in them builds, give them more autonomy.

As your company grows and your time becomes more limited, consider promoting reliable, proven care providers to field supervisors. Have a set system for these visits so that you can teach others to conduct them.

Performance Evaluations

Performance evaluations cover the employees' goal achievement during a specific period. Review new staff after the first 90 days, and then conduct reviews at least annually — preferably semi-annually. The review process is an opportunity for the employee to improve his or her understanding of your expectations and to set additional goals to improve performance. It's an opportunity for the employee to ask questions or express concerns, formally communicate career goals and objectives, and to discuss strengths, weaknesses, and goals between the employee and the company. Finally, you can discuss possible wage increases or decreases based on performance.

You will eventually develop your own style and preferred system for reviews. Initially, the following tips may help:

❖ Communicate the process to the employee. Help him or her understand the review's purpose and desired result.

❖ Always treat the employee with respect. Be friendly, yet professional.

❖ Be objective.

❖ Reinforce positive accomplishments with praise.

❖ Address performance in a non-personal way. Discuss weak areas in terms of improving actions to gain a desired result. Avoid any suggestion of a personal attack; make the discussion about the action and results.

❖ Don't dance around areas that require improvement; address them head-on. Be direct but non-confrontational.

❖ For every criticism, give three praises. Start with praise in one area in which performance is good. Follow by discussing an area that needs improvement. Follow this with two more reinforcements of good performance.

❖ Solicit ideas from the employee on how he or she could improve. Provide the opportunity to think about this, and then record the ideas in a plan of action that you discuss in the next day or two. Then offer your own suggestions.

One week before the review, provide the employee the same employee evaluation form that you will use and ask that it be filled out before the scheduled appointment. This will make plain areas in which you agree or disagree with each other.

When reviewing the employee's performance, consider the full time period covered and not just the most recent memorable event. If performance has been good throughout the period, remember that period as a whole and not only a recent isolated incident.

Continue to interact with your employees so that they feel as though they belong in your organization. Recognize and praise them for the things they do well, treat them with respect, and remember that excellent employees are your company's greatest asset. If you do this, managing your employees will be enjoyable.

Employee Performance Evaluation

EMPLOYEE NAME:

HIRE DATE: / /   **DATE OF EVALUATION:** / /

EVALUATION PERIOD: / / to / /   **LAST REVIEW DATE:** / /

EVALUATORS NAME :   **NEXT REVIEW DATE:** / /

What are the Care Provider's strengths?
_____
_____
_____
_____

What major contributions, accomplishments or improvements has the Care Provider made since last evaluation?
_____
_____
_____
_____

When evaluating individual's performance, refer to the employee's job description and contract for responsibilities and commitments. On the following pages select the rating below that best describes the Care Provider's performance in each area. Total up the points for each category and divide by the number of questions. Grand total all the categories for a single evaluation rating.

1. **Unacceptable:**   Does not meet job requirements and an Action Plan should be written.
2. **Needs Improvement:** Some job requirements are met and performs below the required level. Improvement Action Plan should be written.
3. **Acceptable:**   Consistently performs job requirements at minimum job requirements.
4. **Excellent:**   Consistently performs job requirements at maximum requirements.
5. **Above and Beyond:** Always goes above and beyond job requirements.

RATING	INTEGRITY
	Fulfills commitments as agreed to.
	Is respectful to every client and their family, treating each with dignity and respect.
	Accurately documents services they provided to clients in Care Plan Books.
	Maintains client confidentiality.
	Is honest whenever working with clients and staff.
	Performs job in a positive, cheerful and committed manner.
	Is timely, reliable and committed to fulfilling each assignment with excellence.
	Total Ratings - Divide By 7 =

RATING	PROFESSIONALISM
	Is respectful, considerate and supportive of the company, its staff and clients.
	Maintains clean and professional image, wearing the proper uniform requirements on each and every shift in accordance to their job description.
	Displays a supportive team player attitude with respect to the company, company staff, and clients.
	Displays respect and listens to supervisors, receptive to constructive feedback.
	Maintains confidentiality of clients.
	Maintains confidentiality of personal issues and doesn't discuss them with clients.
	Does not discuss wages or other personal employment details with other staff or clients.
	Communicates employment concerns and issues with direct supervisor, not care providers or clients.
	SubTotal - Divide Total By 8 =

RATING	CONSISTENCY
	Promptly returns calls to the office.
	Consistently uses time reporting systems for each client/visit/shift.
	Promptly communicates client or schedule changes to the office.
	Accurately documents each visit in the client care plans with legible, organized notes.
	Arrives on time or a few minutes early for each client/visit/shift/assignment.
	Schedules are consistently reported to without calling in.
	Total Visits in this period: _____ Total # Days Called In : _____
	Has accepted last minute fill in assignments with short notice.
	SubTotal - Divide Total By 8 =

©2010 HomeCareHowTo.com

157

RATING	CARE DELIVERY
	Displays actions of compassion and understanding to each client.
	Seeks to make a positive difference with each and every client.
	Is positive, helpful and happy in providing care services to each client.
	Continuously looks for ways to help clients.
	Provides services in a way that the client feels they want to be there helping.
	SubTotal - Divide Total By 5 =

RATING	TRAINING
	Has maintained all training requirements for current license (CNA, LVN, etc).
	First Aide & CPR Certified and current.
	Participates in monthly training sessions offered by company.
	Completed Certification Program (HHA, HCA, CNA, etc.)
	Participates in community educational programs.
	SubTotal - Divide Total By 5 =

RATING	ABOVE & BEYOND
	Received a letter of accolades from company.
	Received letter of accolades from a client.
	Volunteers and works for a non-profit, charitable organization, event representing the company.
	Attend a trade show or event representing the company.
	Other: (list)
	SubTotal:

SCORE (Add All Divided Totals)	
Add Above & Beyond	
FINAL SCORE	
Performance Level	

Current Pay Rate	$
New Pay Rate	$

Improvement Action Plan

With a commitment to ongoing training and improvement, the following Improvement Action Plan clearly specifies the goals and actions I've committed to taking to improve my care services.

The Plan will be reviewed and improvements considered again on (date) _____

1. _____
   _____
   _____
   _____
   _____
   _____

2. _____
   _____
   _____
   _____
   _____
   _____
   _____

3. _____
   _____
   _____
   _____
   _____
   _____

4. _____
   _____
   _____
   _____
   _____
   _____

Supervisor Signature: _____ Date:_____

Care Provider Signature: _____ Date:_____

Chapter 8 Review Task List

Upon completing Chapter 8, you should have:

☐ Defined and clearly understand your company's ideal care provider profile.

☐ Set up an applicant response system.

☐ Created an employment application.

☐ Created several employment ads.

☐ Posted and published employment ads.

☐ Set up the application review system.

☐ Set up the applicant screening criteria.

☐ Begun reviewing incoming applications.

☐ Created/modified questions for your interviews.

☐ Conducted several interviews.

☐ Created an applicant assessment rating system.

☐ Conducted reference checks.

☐ Hired your first care provider.

☐ Conducted a background check on each care provider hired.

☐ Set up a care provider training program.

☐ Defined your employee management process.

☐ Set up a client feedback program.

☐ Created a schedule for supervisory schedule for care providers. *(continued next page)*

❏ Set up an employee review process.

CHAPTER 9

OBTAINING CLIENTS

Without clients, you have no business. Until now, you've been working to create the systems that will allow you to serve clients. Now your focus must be on obtaining clients so that you can grow your company to a revenue producing, profitable, rewarding organization.

The Ideal Client

A growing number of people need home care services. You might be tempted to provide every solution for everyone as you build your client base. Don't succumb to this temptation. You will become more frustrated and less focused. Focus on the core niche (for starters, those who require non-medical care). Only after you're operating and profitable should you consider growing into other services if you wish.

To target that niche, define your ideal client. The following list outlines a general snapshot of an ideal client's situation. You may wish to add or subtract certain criteria to best fit your company's desired focus:

❖ Wants to stay in his or her own home but needs help with basic activities to stay there.

❖ Safety concerns such as falling, forgetting the stove is on, not realizing the temperature of the house is hot/cold, getting lost, letting strangers in the house, being paranoid, etc.

❖ Declining eating habits.

❖ No longer bathing, going to the bathroom, or getting dressed properly.

❖ No longer able to keep the home tidy or keep up on home repairs.

❖ Becoming exhausted performing everyday tasks such as laundry or housekeeping.

❖ Forgetting to pay bills, go shopping, or take medication.

❖ Getting lost or confused while walking or driving.

❖ Ambulatory or semi-ambulatory:

  o The client can get around the home and can walk either independently or with some assistance.

  o By focusing on those who are ambulatory or semi-ambulatory, you mitigate the liability that springs from serving clients who are confined to wheelchairs and require transfers to and from the wheelchair.

  o Providing transfers increases the likelihood of injury to employees—increasing workers compensation insurance premiums.

❖ Has family/children who aren't able to assist as often as necessary.

❖ Has family/children who aren't in the area.

❖ No longer drives.

❖ Some have a medical condition that precludes driving; others have decreased vision or declining motor skills; some are not comfortable driving.

❖ Seeks companionship.

❖ Isolation, depression, and anxiety may keep a person from feeling connected.

❖ If family isn't around and the client isn't driving, the client is not getting out very much.

- ❖ Memory loss.

    - o This can include, among many other factors, reversible and non-reversible dementia, Alzheimer's disease, and memory loss due to medication changes.

- ❖ Loss of senses.

- ❖ Vision impairment.

- ❖ Hearing impairment.

- ❖ Smell impairment—this can lead to decreased hygiene.

- ❖ Taste impairment—this increases salt or sugar intake.

- ❖ Motor skill impairment—this inhibits climbing stairs, cooking meals, etc.

- ❖ 65 years of age or older.

- ❖ Lives within your service area.

- ❖ Care providers are usually willing to travel a certain distance from their residence.

- ❖ Recently released from the hospital and needs assistance to recover in their home.

- ❖ A recent fall.

- ❖ Pneumonia.

- ❖ Medication issues—forgetting to take meds, taking meds too often.

- ❖ Diabetic reaction.

- ❖ Physical disabilities.

- ❖ Debilitating medical condition that prevents performing activities around the home.

❖ Diabetes.

❖ Arthritis, osteoporosis.

❖ Muscular dystrophy, Parkinson's disease, ALS (Lou Gehrig's disease), etc.

❖ Respite care.

❖ A family member provides some of the care but needs respite.

❖ Hospice care recipient.

❖ Requires non-medical assistance in conjunction with care provided by the Hospice nursing team.

❖ Able to afford your services.

❖ Has long-term care insurance that pays for your services.

❖ Family/children assist in paying for services.

If any of the above characteristics apply to someone, that person may need help.

How to Obtain Clients

Obtaining clients is a rather simple process if you follow these steps. The amount of time it takes to obtain the clients can vary, though much of it depends upon your efforts.

Create Leads

Creating leads involves marketing your business to your ideal client profile and their influences to find potential clients. Marketing your home care services is a comprehensive topic that will be discussed in detail in the next chapter. For now, here are some basic marketing avenues to promote your services:

Website

A website is as essential to your business as a business card and phone number. Without it you'll lose business. Make your web site findable through Google, Yahoo, and other search directories. Your web developer can help you with this.

Phone Directory Listings

If your phone number is a land line, it should automatically be listed in the Yellow Pages.

Referral Sources

Referral sources—people throughout the elder care community who have regular and direct contact with the elderly—are one of the least expensive and most effective leads because they involve mostly your time and meeting people. It takes only a few key referral sources to provide you with a number of clients.

Chapter 10 covers referral sources in more detail.

Print Ads

Strategically placed print ads can be by far the most expensive form of marketing—but targeted properly, they can result in high-quality leads.

Networking

Joining your local chamber of commerce and community service organizations and attending the events will expose you to influential people. Distribute business cards. Meet new people, ask about what they do, and tell them about what you do.

Receive Inquiries

A lead is anyone who communicates an interest in using your business and falls within the criteria of your ideal-client profile.

Leads come in a number of ways:

1. Phone
2. Email or Web
3. In person

You have only one chance to make a positive first impression. If the inquiry is by email and the inquirer provides a phone number, call him or her immediately. If no phone number is given, reply by email to relay basic information and ask the lead to call you for more details.

When you receive a phone call from a lead, grab a prospect inquiry form (PIF), and ask questions, writing down the information they give. This isn't a formal assessment, so you don't need to know all the details yet. You want to get a general idea of whether the potential client fits your ideal-client profile.

The objectives with the inquiring caller are to:

- ❖ Build some rapport and make the caller feel comfortable with your process.

- ❖ Determine what the situation is and the care needs are.

- ❖ Determine whether the lead fits your ideal-client profile.

- ❖ Learn who makes the final decisions, and get that person's contact information.

- ❖ Determine if the client is able to pay for the services.

- ❖ Schedule an assessment appointment.

- ❖ Get the contact information; name, address, phone number.

❖ Find out how the lead heard about you. Who referred them?

Whatever type of caller, take control of the conversation by asking questions about the situation, listening for the needs, and expressing empathy. Your questions should help you determine the care needs and whether the individual would benefit from your services.

PROSPECT INQUIRY FORM (PIF)

	Inquiry Date:
Client Name:	**Caller Name:**
Client Phone #: ( )	**Caller Phone #:** ( )
Referred By:	**Email Address:**
Relationship to Client:	**Decision Maker:**

Care Situation Notes:

_____

_____

_____

_____

_____

SERVICES NEEDED:

___Companionship	___Couples Care
___Meal Preparation	___Memory Loss Care
___Light Housekeeping	___24-Hour Care
___Errands/ Transportation	___Overnight Stays
___Personal Care / Bathing	___Live-In Care
___Medication Mgmt	___Other:

Is Person Ambulatory? YES | NO
Is Person Continent YES | NO

Currently Using:

___Cane	___Commode
___Disposable Depends	___Hoyer Lift
___Hospice Services	___Scooter
___Hospital Bed	___Hoyer Lift
___Walker	___Wheelchair
___ Other:	___Other:

ASSESSMENT APPOINTMENT

Appt Date: _____
Time: _____
With: _____
Address: _____

Notes:

MARKETING INFO SENT Date Sent ___/___/___

Brochure | Prospect Info Pack (PIP)
Sent to: _____ Client _____ Caller _____ Other
Name: _____
Address: _____
City/State/Zip: _____
Follow Up Date: _____

Set the Assessment Appointment

When it seems that the client would benefit from your services, schedule an assessment interview appointment so you can meet the client and family.

The assessment provides detail that you're not yet aware of—such as the client's physical and mental capacities and an overview of his or her home. This meeting also serves as the opportunity to sign the client service agreement and get a deposit.

"We customize services to each client. To discover which services you need, we do an Assessment Interview. We sit with you in your home and talk about what you'd like to achieve. Together we develop a plan. When would be the best time for you and your family to sit for about an hour? I have time on [these days/these times]—which works best for you? Great! Now, if you can give me your address, I'll put it in my calendar and send you some further information that will help you in the meantime. I look forward to meeting you on [date] at [time]."

Sometimes you may not be able to get an appointment. The client may be exploring other agencies or even just beginning to explore the idea of someone coming in to help. If you're not able to get the appointment, still offer to send the prospect information pack.

After a few days, follow up with a phone call to confirm the receipt of the information and ask if you can be of further help. You don't want to come across as a high-pressure salesperson. Instead, convey that you're willing to help when the time comes.

Send the Prospect Information Pack (PIP)

Remember creating the prospect information packs in Chapter 6: Prepare Prospect Information Packs? Here's where having that set up becomes very useful. Mail one to the client.

If you scheduled the assessment at a time before the potential client would receive the PIP in the mail, bring a few with you to the assessment.

Perform the Assessment

The Assessment is as much about establishing trust and creating a relationship as it is about making the sale. If the prospect thinks that you don't care or that you aren't good at what you do, or if he or she doesn't trust you, you won't make the sale.

The first step in the performing the assessment is to be prepared:

❖ Double-check the appointment time in your calendar.

❖ Call the day before to confirm the appointment and that the decision maker(s) will be present

❖ Have a prospect assessment form (PIF) with the client's name, contact information, and any information you already know filled out in advance.

❖ Bring extra prospect information packs (PIPs) with you.

❖ Prepare and bring several Client Service Agreements with you.

❖ Have a blank care plan book made up. Put the client's name on it in advance.

❖ Be organized. Keep all your paperwork, forms, and care plan book in a tidy briefcase or attaché. The client will notice disorganization.

❖ Dress professionally with clean, ironed clothes.

❖ Arrive right on time, or no more than five minutes early. Never arrive late.

As you make your way to the prospect's home and during the assessment, be thinking of the five step process to the assessment using the acronym **RAPID** to help remember the steps:

Establish **R**apport

Perform the **A**ssessment

Recommend a Care **P**lan

Initiate the Service Agreement

Ask for **D**eposit Payment

Establish Rapport

Upon first meeting your prospect and the family, remember that you're still a stranger. Change that and make a new friend.

As the door is opened for you, smile and show enthusiasm. Greet the prospect and family, and remember each of their names. A person's name is his or her favorite word—use names often throughout the meeting.

As you're shown to the place where you'll be having the meeting (preferably the kitchen table), observe the surroundings of the home. Create conversation using small talk at first. Compliment their home or something about the home.

Take some time to get to know the family. After you've established some connection, explain to them how the assessment will work.

Assess Their Needs

The formal assessment is about you learning as much as you can about the future client. Explain, "The assessment will allow me to find how we can best help you reach what you'd like to accomplish. It involves a series of questions. "Would you mind if I ask you these questions now?" Follow by asking "Do you mind if I take notes?" before taking out your computer or assessment form.

As you begin asking the questions on the prospect assessment form, remember the following:

❖ Sometimes family members will want to answer for the potential client(s). Make an effort to include the person(s) you'll be serving in the whole conversation.

❖ Before the appointment, transfer all the details you've already received over the phone to the assessment form. You'll ask these questions again, but you'll add to the form the additional detail you glean from the assessment.

Be observant of the client and his or her situation:

❖ Observe physical impairments, and ask questions about them.
For example, if you notice the client holds onto walls while walking, ask if he or she uses a walker or has considered using one. Ask what the doctor said about it. How is their vision? Do they get exhausted walking long distance, or do they feel unstable and afraid they will fall?

❖ Be compassionate and understanding throughout the assessment.

Some clients and even their family may be resistant or in denial about the need for help. Be direct with them about their current situation as you observe it.

❖ Ask questions that require more than a yes or no answer. This will give you far more information.

❖ If the client is hearing impaired, lower your voice and speak a little slower. Don't just speak louder.

❖ Learn about the potential client's eating habits. This might reveal potential nutritional deficiencies, indicating the need for your meal planning and preparation services.

Streamlining Your Assessment

If you are using one of the services we recommend as your back office system for scheduling, timekeeping, and overall back office management (eRSP), you'll be pleased to know that a client assessment form is integrated to that system. Instead of bringing the assessment form with you, bring your laptop and fill out the form electronically onsite. Of course, besides your laptop, you'll need a wireless data card/Internet connection to do this. (Note: Never ask to use the prospect's computer or Internet access—it's unprofessional and shows you're unprepared.)

Setting this up in advance will save you time (2-5+ hours) by not having to take the written form back to the office, enter the information, and then determine which care providers are available.

Before you leave, you'll have a good idea of which care providers would be a good fit for the client. You'll need only to contact them to see if they'll be able to do the assignment.

Inquire about recent events that may have contributed to their current situation—e.g., a recent change in medications, a spouse passing away, a recent fall and how it occurred, etc.

Remember to reiterate to the client and family that your care providers perform non-medical care. Should an emergency arise, the care provider's duty is to ensure that the client is safe and secure, then to call 911, and then to call your office. Your office will call the family.

Learn all you can about current elder care issues. The more educated you are about issues such as Alzheimer's disease and dementia, diabetes, geriatric nutrition, community resources, and all that senior care entails, the better you'll be able to provide the very best recommendations for care. The client will feel comfortable and secure knowing that you know what you're doing.

Collect articles that deal with senior issues such as falling, diabetes, driving, Alzheimer's disease, memory loss, etc., and provide the relevant articles to your clients at the Assessment.

CLIENT ASSESSMENT FORM

Personal Information   Date:

First Name	Middle Initial	Last Name

Address	City

State	Zip Code	Telephone

Birth Date / / MM DD YYYY	Age	Gender ☐M ☐F	Height	Weight	Hair Color

Assessment Performed By	Other Parties Present / Title (i/e: family members, Care Manager)

Marital Status   Date of spouse's death
☐ Single   ☐ Married   ☐ Divorced   ☐ Separated   ☐ Widowed

Legal Status
☐ Responsible for Self   ☐ Power of Attorney   ☐ Guardian   ☐ DNR Order -   Location:
Name: Phone Number:

Medical Contact Information

Primary Care Physician	Telephone
Hospital Name & Address	Telephone
Specialist Physician (Specify)	Telephone
Hospital Name & Address	Telephone

Emergency Contact Information

Emergency Contact 1		Relationship	
Address			
City	State	Zip	Telephone

Emergency Contact 2		Relationship	
Address			
City	State	Zip	Telephone

Living Situation

Current Living Situation & Conditions

Significant Events *(Recent or Past)*

Disability History *(When did activities become more difficult)*

Originally From?	Other In-Home Providers? *(Name | Service | Phone #)*
Length of time at current home?	NOTES
Any Children?	Any Pets? *(Animal Type & Names)*
Is Family/Children in the Area?	Care Required for Pets?
Visitation Frequency	Veterinarian Contact Info

ACTIVITIES

Hobbies	Previous Career/Occupation
Favorite Activities Currently Doing	Favorite Activities But Can't Do
Ongoing Social Activities	Clubs/Organization Membership
Friends & Visitors	Visitation Frequency

DRIVING

☐ Currently able to drive	Vehicle Registration current? ☐ YES ☐ NO
☐ Unable to drive. *(check ONE below)* ☐ Client's car used for Transportation ☐ Caregiver's car used for Transportation	Auto Insurance Company Policy # Date of last service

FUNCTIONAL ASSESSMENT

Levels of Assistance:
  0=Independent – Completes the task independently
  3=Minimum Assistance – Occasional assistance or supervision may be necessary
  6=Moderate Assistance – Assistance or supervision is always necessary
  9=Maximum Assistance – Totally dependent on others

1. For each activity check the box indicating the assistance needed.
2. If assistance is needed, indicate the source of help *(be specific: spouse, family, friend, paid help, volunteer, professional)*
3. In the comments indicate the type of assistance provided and how often it's provided. Indicate if client needs further help.

ACTIVITIES OF DAILY LIVING

Activity	Ind. 0	Min. Assist 3	Mod. Assist 6	Max Assist 9	Primary Source of Help	Comments / Other Sources
Eating	☐	☐	☐	☐		
Bathing	☐	☐	☐	☐		
Grooming	☐	☐	☐	☐		
Dressing	☐	☐	☐	☐		
Toileting	☐	☐	☐	☐		
Mobility	☐	☐	☐	☐		
Transferring	☐	☐	☐	☐		

INSTRUMENTAL ACTIVITIES OF DAILY LIVING

Activity	Ind. 0	Min. Assist 3	Mod. Assist 6	Max Assist 9	Primary Source of Help	Comments / Other Sources
Laundry	☐	☐	☐	☐		
Meal Preparation	☐	☐	☐	☐		
Light Housework	☐	☐	☐	☐		
Heavy Housework	☐	☐	☐	☐		
Shopping/Errands	☐	☐	☐	☐		
Transportation	☐	☐	☐	☐		
Medication Mgmt	☐	☐	☐	☐		

Adaptive Equipment	Has	Has but Doesn't Use	Needs	Comments
Cane/Crutches/Walker	☐	☐	☐	
Wheelchair *(manual / power)*	☐	☐	☐	
Toilet Equip. *(commode / seat)*	☐	☐	☐	
Bathing Equip *(seat / grab bars)*	☐	☐	☐	
Hospital Bed *(power / manual)*	☐	☐	☐	
Hoyer Lift *(power / manual)*	☐	☐	☐	
Other:	☐	☐	☐	
Dentures	☐	☐	☐	
Diabetic Supplies	☐	☐	☐	
Incontinence Products	☐	☐	☐	
Medical Phone Alert	☐	☐	☐	
Other:	☐	☐	☐	

MEDICAL DIAGNOSIS

Diagnosed medical conditions/diseases

Memory *(describe)*		Wanders
☐ Dementia		☐ Uses electronic alert system
		Company:
☐ Alzheimer's		☐ Other

Drug Use/Abuse *(describe)*

Prescription Medications

Pharmacy Location		Phone #	
Prescription	Dosage	Time to Take	Doctor
Prescription	Dosage	Time to Take	Doctor
Prescription	Dosage	Time to Take	Doctor
Prescription	Dosage	Time to Take	Doctor
Prescription	Dosage	Time to Take	Doctor
Prescription	Dosage	Time to Take	Doctor
Prescription	Dosage	Time to Take	Doctor
Prescription	Dosage	Time to Take	Doctor
Prescription	Dosage	Time to Take	Doctor

Over the Counter Medications

Medication	Dosage	Frequency	Notes
Medication	Dosage	Frequency	Notes
Medication	Dosage	Frequency	Notes
Medication	Dosage	Frequency	Notes
Pharmacy Location		Phone #	

Medication Notes

Nutrition

Typical Current Meals

Breakfast	Lunch	Dinner

Snacks

Favorite Foods:

			Special Notes/ Nutrition Concerns
Eats fewer than 2 meals per day	YES	NO	
Eats few fruits, vegetables or milk products	YES	NO	
Drinks beer, wine or liquor daily/regularly	YES	NO	
Has tooth or mouth problems that makes it difficult to eat	YES	NO	
Has gained/lost 10 pounds in past 6 months	YES	NO	

Sleep Patterns

Wakes	Bedtime
Daytime Naps	Nocturnal Wakening

Fall Risk Screening

1.	How many times have you fallen in the past year?		
2.	Are you worried you might have a fall?	☐ Not at all ☐ Somewhat	☐ A little ☐ Very
3.	Do you limit activities now because of fall-related concerns?	☐ Never ☐ Sometimes	☐ Occasionally ☐ Often

If client has NOT fallen in the past year, skip questions 4 & 5 below.

4.	Where have you fallen?	☐ Getting in & out of bed ☐ Outside the home ☐ Between the bed & the bathroom ☐ Other:	☐ Bathroom ☐ Kitchen
5.	Can you say what makes you more likely to fall?	☐ Feeling dizzy/lightheaded ☐ Walking in darkness ☐ Walking on certain surfaces ☐ Stairs ☐ Other:	☐ Getting up too quickly ☐ Certain Shoes ☐ Turns ☐ Dim Lighting

Insurance

Long Term Care Coverage? ☐ YES ☐ NO	Company:
Policy #:	Phone #:
	Contact Agent:

180

Recommend a Care Plan

After you've completed all the questions on the prospect assessment form, review your notes and determine which services you think the client needs. Identify the tasks that the prospective client is already doing very well.

Before you start telling the client what you think he or she needs, talk about areas in which they are doing well. This provides encouragement and reduces defensiveness as you begin proposing the areas in which you can assist.

In a positive manner, outline and discuss the tasks for which you think the client needs assistance. Your goal is to present the plan without making the client feel inadequate.

As you present the recommended care plan, pull out the client's care plan book. Record each service you'll be performing. Then have the client sign the prospect assessment form and the proposed care plan form.

PLAN OF CARE : NON-MEDICAL IN HOME CARE

Date: _____

Client Name:			Client Phone #:
Address:	City:	State:	Zip:
Diagnosis:		Allergies/Restrictions:	
Age:	Birthdate:	DNR: ☐ Yes ☐ No	Height:	Weight:
Type of Service:	Service Days:	Service Hours:	

COMPANION CARE

☐ **Companionship & Safety**
  ☐ Per visit ☐ Per request
  ☐ Reading   ☐ Hobbies
  ☐ Mental Stimulation
  ☐ Alzheimers
  ☐ Dementia
  ☐ Other:

☐ **Meal Preparation:**
  ☐ Per visit ☐ Per request
  ☐ Cook meals:
  ☐ Assist with Feeding
  ☐ Nothing by mouth
  ☐ Dietary restrictions:
  ☐ Favorite Foods:
  ☐ Notes:

☐ **Light Housekeeping:**
  ☐ Per visit ☐ Per request
  ☐ Vacuuming:
    AREAS:
  ☐ Dusting:
    AREAS:
  ☐ Make Bed:
    NOTES:
  ☐ Tidy Common Areas:
    AREAS:

☐ **Laundry:**
  ☐ Per visit ☐ Per request
  ☐ Wash   ☐ Dry
  ☐ Ironing:
  ☐ Change Bed Linens

☐ **Medication:**
  ☐ Medication Reminders
  ☐ Self Managed
  ☐ Details/Notes:

☐ **Transportation:**
  ☐ Client vehicle
  ☐ Employee vehicle
  ☐ Accompany client if family drives
  ☐ Special Instructions:

PERSONAL CARE

☐ **Bathing**
  ☐ None   ☐ Shower
  ☐ Sponge bath   ☐ Tub bath
  ☐ Shampoo   ☐ Comb
  ☐ Monitoring Only ☐ Stndby/Asst
  ☐ Shaving (electric shaver only)
  ☐ Other:

☐ **Dressing:**
  ☐ Total Assistance
  ☐ Partial Assistance
  ☐ Assist w/ socks & shoes

☐ **Elimination**
  ☐ Per visit ☐ Per request
  ☐ Check bowel movement
  ☐ Change disposables/pad if soiled
  ☐ Incontinent of ☐ urine ☐ bowel
  ☐ Foley catheter
  ☐ Foley cath care with soap/water
  ☐ External catheter
  ☐ Notes/Other:

☐ **Ambulation / Assist / Transfer**

  ☐ Ambulatory   ☐ Bedridden
  ☐ Walker/Cane   ☐ Wheelchair

  ☐ Walks with Assistance
  ☐ Standby / Assist   ☐ Fall risk
  ☐ Needs lifting from bed/chair
  ☐ Partial or Full Transfers
  ☐ Reposition/Notes:

☐ **Oral Care**
  ☐ None
  ☐ Brush teeth
  ☐ Dentures?:
    ☐ Yes ☐ No
  ☐ Other:
  ☐ Other:

  ☐ Other:

  ☐ Other:

SAFETY

☐ **Safety Measures**
  ☐ Siderails
  ☐ Grab bars
  ☐ Pathways clear
  ☐ Emergency Alert System
  ☐ Other:

☐ **Equipment & Supplies**
  ☐ None   ☐ Commode
  ☐ Walker   ☐ Urinal
  ☐ Cane   ☐ Hospital Bed
  ☐ Wheelchair   ☐ Hoyer Lift
  ☐ Gait Belt   ☐ Incontinence
  ☐ Gloves   products used
  ☐ Other:

☐ **Other:**
  ☐ Smoking:
  ☐ Alcohol Use:
  ☐

☐ **Pet Care:**
  ☐ Required Pet Care:
  ☐ Pets   Type:
  ☐ Describe:
    Pet's Name(s):

☐ **Mental Status:**

☐ **Hearing:**
☐ **Vision:**

☐ **Notes:**

Sun	From	To
Mon	From	To
Tue	From	To
Wed	From	To
Thu	From	To
Fri	From	To
Sat	From	To

©2010 HomeCareHowTo.com

182

Initiate the Client Service Agreement

Review the proposed care plan form, and estimate how many hours per week and month your services will be needed. Determine the rate that applies to this client, and explain your rates to the client. Calculate the total weekly and monthly amounts you'll be charging. Then ask: "Is there anything that would prevent you from investing this amount to reach your goals and make your life more enjoyable?"

Should the client object to the price, find out what would work for the client. For example, if you suggest visits five or six days a week and the client says that that is not affordable, propose two or three days week. Then negotiate an agreement that works for both the client and you.

Should You Collect a Deposit?

The retainer deposit you collect serves a couple purposes:

* It commits the client to your services as you put the time and effort into placing a care provider.

* It helps the company fund the payroll that you'll be paying the care provider before the client pays the first invoice.

When you've reached an agreement, have the client sign the client service agreement, and collect the retainer deposit.

Once the agreement is signed and the deposit is in hand, let the client know that you'd like to get started immediately. Set a time to introduce the new care provider. Thank the client for the opportunity to be able to help, and end the meeting.

HOME CARE SERVICES AGREEMENT

Client Last Name:	First Name:	M.I.:	Client ID No.:
Financially Responsible Person (If other than Client)	Relationship:	Phone:	Email:

I, the undersigned, hereby make the following agreement regarding care services to be provided by ABC Home Care Services, located at 123 Anywhere Ave, Taylor, WA 98765. I understand that a photocopy of this agreement shall be as valid as the original.

AGREEMENT FOR SERVICES

This agreement sets forth the terms of our engagement and the nature of our services to be provided and your responsibilities in connection with such services.

ABC Home Care Services is a provider of non-medical in-home companion care to the elderly who require assistance with daily living activities. I wish to engage ABC HOME CARE SERVICES to provide a caregiver at your home during mutually agreed upon advanced scheduled times. The times and services to be performed are thoroughly outlined in The Care Plan.

Our business relationship is strictly between you and ABC HOME CARE SERVICES Home Care. ABC Home Care Services manages and supervises all aspects of employment of our staff including employment, scheduling, coordination, placement, reviews, payroll, taxes, insurance, worker's compensation and discipline. Communications, all schedule changes, questions, comments, complaints regarding our services and/or staff should be directed to ABC HOME CARE SERVICES Home Care's main office.

I understand that I will be charged the following rate for services rendered based on the level of care provided and hours/visits/days worked, which is: _____ per **HOUR | VISIT | DAY**. I understand that I will be charged time and one-half for all national holidays including and not limited to: New Year's Eve, New Year's Day, Martin Luther King Jr. Day, Easter Day, Memorial Day, Independence Day, Labor Day, Thanksgiving Day, Christmas Eve and Christmas Day. Federal and state law requires employers to pay employees overtime for hours worked in excess of 8 hours per day and/or 40 hours per week. In the event that a caregiver is specifically requested by the client to work longer than 40 hours per week, the overtime rate will be charged at time and one-half.

ABC HOME CARE SERVICES understands that clients schedule and needs change over time. In the event I need to change or cease ABC Home Care Services services, I will provide ABC HOME CARE SERVICES at least twenty-four (24) hours advance cancellation notice. Except in medical emergency situations, I understand by providing less than 24 hours notice to ABC HOME CARE SERVICES , I will be invoiced and responsible for the normally scheduled visit.

MILEAGE

I understand that mileage may be charged if an employee uses his/her personal vehicle to transport/run errands for me. ABC HOME CARE SERVICES warrants that each Caregiver providing driving services is validly licensed to drive with proper insurance coverage. To cover the cost of gasoline, wear and tear, and insurance costs, I will be charged the current year federal tax rate ($.50/per mile in 2010) beyond the included 10 total miles per visit. I understand the federal tax rates may change at the start of each calendar year and updated rates are available by contacting ABC HOME CARE SERVICES. If I authorize the use of my automobile for errands and incidental transportation in connection with our care services, I agree to carry insurance and authorization is needed from the client to the agency prior to the use of your car. ABC HOME CARE SERVICES insurance does not cover loss or damage caused by caregiver employees operating the client's owned or leased vehicle.

Page 1 of 3

184

HOME CARE SERVICES AGREEMENT

FINANCIAL RESPONSIBILITY

I understand that by signing below, I am responsible for payment of services, including services not paid by my insurer, if applicable. As a service to me upon request, ABC HOME CARE SERVICES will submit insurance claims to insurance companies, but this does not relieve me of my financial responsibility. I understand that service Invoices are sent every two weeks and payable upon receipt. Caregivers are paid regularly and prompt payment of invoices is necessary. I understand that any invoice(s) that become past due in excess of 10 days will be assessed a late fee and begin to accrue interest at the rate of 1.85% per month.

To place a qualified caregiver in your home and begin services, a *refundable retainer deposit* equal to the amount of two weeks estimated services is required. The deposit amount is calculated by (estimated hours per week) X (Service Rate) X 2 weeks. If the amount of service hours should increase, an additional deposit equal to the amount of the increased service hours over two weeks may be required.

Estimated hours per week: _____

Service Rate: $_____   Per Hour   Per Day

                                          X 2 Weeks

Total Retainer Deposit $_____

Two convenient payment options. Please initial next to your choice:

1) _____ Credit Card: Please charge my credit card for the refundable retainer deposit and each invoice. An itemized invoice will be mailed every two weeks with the current charges to the card with a receipt for the transaction. If the credit card expires, becomes invalid or is otherwise not accepted, I will provide an updated credit card or make alternate payment arrangements immediately.

Credit Card Type:	Name on Account:	Account Number:
Exp Date:	Address of Account Holder:	Security Code (3 digits on back of card):

2) _____ Check: I will make invoice payments by check upon receipt of each invoice. An itemized invoice will be mailed every two weeks with the current charges. The refundable retainer deposit in the amount of $_____ (2 weeks of estimated service) is included. When services are no longer required, the deposit amount will be credited to any outstanding balances and a final statement will be mailed with any outstanding balances. In the event that payment for an invoice isn't received within 15 days, the retainer deposit will be applied to any outstanding invoices to bring the account current and I am still responsible for payment to bring the retainer deposit current.

In the event it becomes necessary to collect this account, I agree to pay all costs incurred to collecting the debt, including late fees, interest, legal and court fees.

VERIFICATION OF SERVICE

I understand that each employee who renders service will require use of my telephone to "Clock-In" at the beginning of any visit and "Clock-Out" at the end of any visit using a toll-free number which connects to ABC HOME CARE SERVICES 's Telephony System and verifies the employees physical location by use of caller ID. I understand this digitally accurate, computerized time and management system is used to prepare bills and process payroll. I agree to allow use of my phone for registering the start and end of each visit. I further

Page 2 of 3

185

HOME CARE SERVICES AGREEMENT

understand that my signature authorizes my invoices to be calculated and detail billed based on ABC HOME CARE SERVICES 's Telephony System.

HIRING OF EMPLOYEES

ABC Home Care Services takes great pride and effort to finding and retaining the very best Employees. Recruiting and retaining the very best staff takes time, patience, resources, extensive effort, training and cost. We invest in our staff because we believe clients deserve the very best.
In the honor and spirit of our relationship, I agree not to make private arrangements with or employ any employee of ABC HOME CARE SERVICES directly or indirectly in any manner for a period of one year following the last day ABC HOME CARE SERVICES rendered services to me, regardless of employee status at ABC HOME CARE SERVICES. If I choose to hire a caregiver directly or make private arrangements away from ABC HOME CARE SERVICES, directly or indirectly, I understand I will be charged the fair rate of $5,000.00 as liquidated damages, payable immediately to compensate and reimburse us for the cost of hiring and training of employee expenses, and lost income. I understand that I should never pay employees of ABC HOME CARE SERVICES directly, make any loans, gifts of or advance(s) of money to them.

ABC HOME CARE's mission is to offer Excellence in non-medical home care and is committed to offering superior quality service to its clients. I understand that ABC HOME CARE SERVICES assigns staff based on client needs and considerations related directly to the care/services provided. ABC HOME CARE SERVICES will make every effort to fulfill the service request but does not guarantee uninterrupted service 100% of the time. I understand that despite all efforts, there may be an interruption of services due to factors beyond the control of ABC HOME CARE SERVICES. If you need to voice a grievance or offer suggestions for improving, please notify us at ABC Home Care Services (333) 444-5555. Our staff will take immediate action to resolve all problems brought to their attention. We appreciate the opportunity to be of service to you and look forward to a long-lasting relationship.

I agree to keep any cash and checks, jewelry and other valuables in a secure and locked place. For everyone's benefit, I agree on behalf of the care recipient and the family, that a thorough investigation be conducted on any missing items, articles or valued possessions or accusations there of.

Either party may cancel this Agreement at any time with seven days advance notice to the other party in writing. This does not apply to emergency medical situations such as hospitalization. If services are interrupted for any reason, you agree to give us a minimum of seven days notice to avoid forfeiture of the retainer deposit. ABC HOME CARE SERVICES has the absolute right, without limitation or penalty; to stop all work immediately in the event there are disputes and/or delinquent fees due ABC HOME CARE SERVICES .

The foregoing is in accordance with our understanding and we hereby agree to it's terms and conditions.

Client Signature	Date
Address	
Financially Responsible Party Signature (if Other Than Client)	Date
ABC Home Care Services Representative Signature	Date

Page 3 of 3

186

Identify & Assign The Care Provider

The suggested software systems mentioned in Chapter 6: Contact Management Systems include client and care provider scheduling. Now is the time that you'll appreciate that software.

Enter the client's information into the system using the information you gathered from the assessment form. This includes all the care needs, visit days and times, and medical diagnosis information.

Assuming you've entered all the care providers you've hired into the system, the software program will find care provider(s) with the skills, availability, and serviceable location for your new client. If the client needs visits a few

Assigning Care Providers

Make absolutely sure you've confirmed that each care provider has accepted the assignment. If any questions or hesitations arise, wait until you have complete confirmation before notifying the client.

Don't wait too long for a care provider to call you back to fill an assignment. Your goal is to staff this assignment so you need to create Plan A and Plan B in the event you don't hear back from that "perfect fit" care provider.

days a week, one care provider should be able to cover the shifts consistently. A client who requires more than eight hours of care per day or needs care seven days per week, will need several care providers in order to prevent care provider burnout and paying overtime wages.

If you haven't set up the back office software system and you're going by memory or spreadsheet, then you'll still need to match the client's requested schedule with an available care provider(s). Identify the available care providers, and then match skill sets with the client's needs. For example, can the care provider serve the client's location, can they assist with continence care, are they excellent cooks, and will they help bathe the client? Doing this manually is a chore. Software does all this matching for you.

Also consider personalities. Ideally, several care providers' skills and schedule availability will meet the client's needs. Your objective is to fill the assignment with the best care provider possible considering the personalities and the client's best interests.

Once you've located the best candidates for the client, begin calling the care provider(s). Sometimes the best care provider can't fill the role, so have a backup or two. As soon as you've confirmed that a care provider will accept the assignment, set a time to meet with him or her to discuss the client, care plan, and care objectives.

Call the client to explain who will be his or her care provider(s). Be complimentary of the care provider(s), and set a time to introduce them to the client before beginning services. Some may ask to meet the care provider(s) several times before starting actual services.

Create the Care Plan Book

A Care Plan Book is the communication tool that holds not only the care plan but the information from the most recent assessment, emergency procedures, the documentation of services from the care provider(s), and documentation about each visit. The care provider, client, and the client's family use this book to keep everyone informed about the client's ongoing care. This book should stay in the client's home at all times.

The book itself should be a heavy-duty 3-ring binder with a clear plastic top pocket cover allowing you to insert an 81/2" x 11" page that has the client's name, address, and phone number along and your company's logo and phone number.

The binder has five sections, separated by divider tabs, so that the essential information can be found quickly.

The five sections include:

1. The Care Plan
2. The Assessment
3. Emergency Steps

4. Elder Home Safety Checklist
5. Care Documentation

The Care Plan:

The most recent up to date care plan is placed at the front of this section. Using the care plan completed at the assessment appointment, complete any details that may not have been added at the assessment. Print out a fully completed form. As updates are made to the care plan, they will be placed on top. Including the previous care plans allows for all involved in the care to review progress and see where the client is progressing or regressing.

The Assessment:

Using the all the information learned about the client at the assessment, complete a detailed assessment form in computer format. Refer to your notes that may not have been entered at the time of the assessment. The most recent assessment is placed on the top of the section, with previous assessments underneath.

Emergency Steps:

This section outlines the steps to perform if an emergency occurs and 911 is called. While the emergency steps are much the same for each client, this section outlines client specific information.

Elder Home Safety Checklist:

Each item on the checklist should be marked as being performed and completed. In some cases, the client will specifically request an item on the checklist not be completed. That item should be noted to that effect.

Care Documentation:

At the end of each visit (and if necessary, during) the care provider should document what took place during the visit. This includes checking off the tasks completed and brief notes of observations about the client care notes. Notes can also be left to and from family members about the client's care. The notes should be objective, succinct, and legible.

Physicians and family members can use the documentation to identify patterns of changes in the client, leading to the adjustments in services or changes in the care plan itself.

The care plan book should be kept out of plain view to prevent casual viewing by people not involved in the client's care. Discuss the best location with the client, making sure that the care provider, family member(s), and client all know where it will be consistently stored. A kitchen cupboard is a convenient location—easy to access in a central location and close to a counter or table for writing notes into it.

Review Care Plan with the Care Provider

The meeting with the care provider is essential prior to his or her meeting the client. Have the client's care plan book with you when you discuss the care plan with the care provider.

The meeting with your care provider shouldn't take more than an hour. Begin the meeting by objectively reviewing the details about the client's current physical and mental conditions. Explain the family situation and how involved they will be. Explain the care plan and what the planned objectives are for the client.

In your review of what will be expected, pay attention to the care provider's words and body language. Confront any indication of discomfort. It's better to uncover potential problems now than have the care provider not meet expectations later.

If the care provider has are any questions about the care, address them at this meeting. If you can't answer some of these questions, make notes and follow up quickly with the client so that you can answer the care provider's questions before he or she meets the client.

Introduce the Care Provider and Begin Services

The objective of the introduction appointment is about the client meeting the care provider, establishing a rapport and feeling comfortable with each other. Many times the client has not had someone come into their home to help them and it's a dramatic lifestyle change so understand the client may be still be apprehensive about the services. Some clients may need several meetings before feeling comfortable having the care provider beginning services.

The introduction is smoothest if you—the one who performed the assessment—conducts it. After the initial introduction, allow for the care provider to interact with the client a bit. Experienced care providers usually have the skills to break the ice and make the client feel at ease. Pay attention to the interaction from the start—your observations are the first step to the ongoing reviews you'll be conducting with the employee.

After the two appear to be comfortable with one another, introduce the care plan book, and review the book's contents with the client and care provider together. Since you've already briefed the care provider about the care plan before the meeting, the review is about making sure the care plan meets the client's understanding and expectations.

Begin Client Follow-Ups

If the client is receiving services several times each week, call after a few days—after three visits at the most—to find out how the client is feeling about the services. If the client receives services only twice a week, follow up after the second visit.

Ask questions to flesh out any questions or concerns about the care being provided. By following up after the first few visits, it will allow you to discover if care is sufficient or needs to be adjusted.

Perform Ongoing Visits and Assessments

Follow-up visits and ongoing assessments are essential in developing long-term relationships with clients.

Plan visits after the first and second week of service. These visits will reveal how well the care plan developed, whether it's meeting the client's needs, and if adjustments need to be made. It also serves as a supervisory visit to ensure the care provider is providing exactly what the care plan calls for and if adjustments need to be made.

If the first two visits reveal the necessity for significant care plan adjustments or that the care provider is not meeting expectations, conduct a third meeting with the client and family to ensure that all of the goals are being met.

Note that the first week or two of care can often require great adjustment for clients. Home care services may be new to them, and they might still hesitate to accept help. As the client begins to trust the care provider, the more he or she is willing to let someone else care for them.

If by the third week or after many visits a client still reports dissatisfaction, you need to address the issue. Personalities may be conflicting, the care provider may not be meeting the expectations, or the client may be adamant against the services. If applicable, contact the family member who is the main point of contact to discuss the situation. Often others involved in the care will provide the insight to what's really going on. If the problem is a personality clash or a failure to meet expectations, changing care providers may be the solution. Or perhaps the care provider is doing just one thing wrong and can fix the problem.

Clients' needs change over time. You need to be aware of these changes; monthly visits should help you see them. These visits also show the client that you're truly involved in their well being.

Plan to schedule monthly visits; also plan for some unscheduled visits in between. Unscheduled visits can be especially revealing as to whether the care provider is performing properly. A care provider who knows that you'll show up unexpectedly knows that you are keeping tabs on his or her performance. If he or she works hard only when a visit is scheduled and backs off when you are not expected, you will see the difference during your unscheduled visits.

Chapter 9 Review Task List

Upon completing Chapter 9, you should have:

❑ Created an ideal-client profile and clearly understand who your ideal client is.

❑ An understanding of the steps to obtaining clients.

❑ Created the initial systems for creating leads.

❑ Created the process for incoming leads.

❑ Created a prospect inquiry form (PIF).

❑ An understanding of the assessment process.

❑ Created/modified the assessment form.

❑ Made several care plan books to have stock for clients.

❑ Created the process for assigning care providers to a new client.

❑ Created the process for beginning services to a new client.

❑ Created the process for client follow-ups.

❑ Created a schedule for ongoing visits and assessments.

CHAPTER 10

MARKETING YOUR SERVICES

Marketing and sales is the fuel that builds your business. How you market and sell dictates how quickly your company grows. This requires daily work on improving your marketing and sales while implementing what you learn through reading books on sales and marketing.

Plan and Prepare for Marketing

Just as your business plan is a fluid entity, so is your marketing plan and strategy. It will change along with different variables such as the economy, laws, community needs and goals.

Recommended Books

These timeless books should be in every entrepreneur's library:

The Greatest Secret *by Og Mandino*

Think and Grow Rich *by Napolean Hill*

Success Through a Positive Mental Attitude *by Napolean Hill*

See You at the Top *by Zig Ziglar*

Success Begins with Believing in Yourself!

Before any marketing or sales plan can be effective, you must believe in yourself. People can sense if you believe in what you're doing. Even if your presentation or assessment techniques need work, belief in yourself will show and can make the sale.

Set Goals

Without a target to aim for, you won't push yourself. The goals you set should be believable and just a little bit beyond—if you set them beyond and fall just short of achieving them, you haven't failed. Push yourself to take the action required to meet them. If you set the goals too low and hit them every time, you may be setting goals much lower than your capabilities.   When you set your goals, make them **SMART**:

Specific
When your goals are specific, you can create steps to make them achievable. Ask yourself the six W questions: who, what, when, where, which, and why.

Who is involved?
What specifically do I want to accomplish?
When will I accomplish them—specific period of time?
Where will I accomplish them?
Which constraints, resources, and requirements will be needed?
Why do I want to accomplish this goal? What reasons, purpose, or benefits will I receive by reaching the goal?

Measurable
Set specific criteria for measuring progress toward reaching your goals. When you measure your progress, you stay on track and

GOAL SETTING

Learn better goal setting with the following books:

Goals by Zig Ziglar

The New Dynamics Of Goal Setting
by Dennis Waitley

The Ultimate Goals Program: How to Get Everything You Want
by Brian Tracy

For your convenience, go to HomeCareHowTo.com and find the books quickly.

meet your goal.

One way to measure your goals is by reverse engineering. Reverse engineering means looking at the end of the goal and determining what numbers will be required to reach to accomplish the goals—then working those numbers backwards into monthly, weekly, and daily action steps.

Achievable

You can reach almost any goal when you plan your steps wisely and set a reasonable timeframe. Seemingly unreachable goals eventually become reachable—not because the goals shrink but because you build your skills and efforts to match them. But be honest with yourself. If you set out to make $500,000 this year and you're not willing to do the work necessary to do so, you're setting yourself up for failure.

Realistic
If you truly believe that you can reach a goal, the goal is probably realistic. A goal can be both high and realistic; only you can determine just how high your goal should be.

Timed

If you don't set a timeframe, you don't experience the urgency to complete. If you set a specific date, you will find yourself working toward the completion within that timeframe.

Now that you've set your goals, tell someone you trust. Give him or her a list of your specific goals, and ask to be held accountable. Accountability should be tied to reward or penalty. Create a reward for achieving specific goals and a consequence for falling short. The reward should be strong enough to motivate you to want to continue. The consequence should be strong enough that you don't want to do it.

Measure the Results

What's worth doing is worth measuring. The only way to know if you're getting results is to track and measure things. Measuring will tell you how well your business plan is working, how effective a marketing campaign is, what marketing efforts are getting the best results, and which marketing efforts need to be adjusted or discontinued. This applies to every area of your business—the number of employment applications you get back from your Help Wanted ads, the daily contacts you need to make, the ongoing supervisory visits, and so on.

Tracking the effectiveness of a marketing campaign is done by measuring leads—where they came from and how many of them turn into sales. Meanwhile, keep track of leads that don't turn into sales so you can continue to keep in contact with them should they need your services in the future.

Now you understand the importance of asking this single question at the end of the prospect inquiry: "How did you hear about us?" This will help you track and measure the success of each marketing column. Continuing an ad that doesn't get results, for example, doesn't make sense. If something isn't working, change it.

After you've asked that question, record the answer—ideally in a contact management system that allows you to set up the different stages of the sales process.

The Value of a Client

A client's monetary value is an essential number to know. It determines how much you should spend to acquire a client in order to be profitable.

Calculate the number by taking the average client's net profit over a period of time. For example, if your average home care client is using your services 15 hours per week for 6 months and the average net profit from this client is $450 per month (a total of $2,700 over the six months), you can spend $2,600 to acquire the client and still realize a $100 profit after six months.

On the other hand, if an ad campaign is costing you $3,000 every six months and brings only one client, you're losing money. The ad campaign may pick up over the next six months, but it may not. As you track the effectiveness of your campaigns, drop or change the campaigns that are losing money. Forget the "exposure" that many newspaper salespeople will try to sell you on; put the money into marketing efforts that have worked for you.

Client Acquisition Cost

To calculate client acquisition cost (the amount of money you spend on marketing and administration required to obtain a client), add the marketing and administrative costs and divide by the total number of your new clients within the period of your costs incurred. This will give you a good idea of where your profitability percentage is. If your client acquisition costs exceed the value of your client, you need to adjust something.

<u>Client Acquisition Cost Example:</u>	
Total cost of marketing ads for 6 months	$8000
Total cost of administrative time/office	$1300
Total Marketing & Admin Costs	$9300
Total new clients for 6 months	19
$9300/19 = $489	
Total Acquisition Cost per Client	$489

In the above example, the break-even point for each client is $489 in gross profit from services. If the average client requires 15 hours per week at $18/hour and the gross profit margin is 30%, it will take 6.03 weeks of service before breaking even. If a client has more hours, this would take considerably less time.

As you arrive at your numbers, look at your marketing efforts to determine where you can improve effectiveness and reduce the client acquisition costs. Concentrate on the areas that are working, and adjust the areas that aren't.

Creating Your Leads List

A leads list—one of the most valuable assets your company can create and build on—is a list of the prospective clients that meet your ideal-client profile. Creating a leads list allows you to target your marketing efforts to individuals who may currently need or may need your services in the future.

Creating your leads list involves the following:

- ❖ Identifying your ideal-client profile (which you've already done).

- ❖ Setting up your contact management software.

- ❖ Obtaining prospects who fit the ideal-client profile.

- ❖ Adding and tracking prospects with the list.

Identify Your Ideal-Client Profile

In Chapter 9 we discussed who your ideal client is. Follow what your ideal client profile is as closely as possible. Keeping your marketplace narrow will bring far greater success. Learn to say no to the care that falls outside your area of expertise. When you specialize in a smaller niche, people consider you the expert.

Set Up Your Contact Management Software

You need to have a system in place to manage your contact list. The contact relationship management (CRM) helps you manage your relationships with contacts of prospective clients and clients themselves.

Integrating the backend eRSP system simplifies the tracking of your leads from first call through the sales process. It's already built in—you customize it with your sales process. If you have chosen something other than the eRSP system, consider one of the following contact management software programs:

Salesforce.com — www.salesforce.com — An Internet based sales tracking software. Very customizable, and since it's web-based you'll have access to it at all times with an Internet connection.

Sage ACT! — www.act.com — This is a client based software and is customizable as well. It allows you to set up your sales process, also called the Sales Funnel. You can do reports, run mailing lists, and so much more.

FreeCRM.com — www.freecrm.com — A free web-based contact management software. Features and support are limited with the free version; however, you can upgrade if you need additional features. This is a great inexpensive solution upfront.

When purchasing your CRM, consider your long-term needs. As your leads list and client list grows, so will your CRM requirements. Once you set up one system, changing to a different program will take a lot of time, effort, and resources. If at all possible, strongly consider a CRM that is integrated with the back office systems designed specifically for home care.

Finding Leads That Fit the Ideal Client Profile

Generating a list of prospects generally requires your own marketing efforts or purchasing targeted contacts outright.

Marketing

As you begin networking and implementing marketing campaigns, prospect inquiry calls (a.k.a. leads) will begin coming in. After each prospect inquiry is entered into your CRM, it starts being tracked with all the other inquiries. The inquiries that don't turn into sales are still prospects, and you should continue to keep in touch with them as you do with clients.

Purchase

The other way to generate a list of leads is buying lead lists. Buying a list lets you be selective and personalize the criteria of individuals you're seeking. Thousands of available lists classify consumers according to a variety of demographic criteria—e.g., age, income, buying habits, house values, etc.

Here are a few national providers to get you started if you want to purchase lists—or lease or rent them, if that better fits your budget. You can find many more by Googling "Leads Lists." Research the one that fits best your needs.

Go Leads — www.goleads.com

Info USA — www.infousa.com

List of Leads—www.listofleads.com

Cactus Mailing—www.cactusmailing.com

Mailing List Shop—www.mailinglistshop.com

Once you've purchased a list, add its contents to your CRM under the classification of the purchased list. When people call, you want to know where the leads originated from. Actual leads will fit several of the criteria of your ideal-client list— such as age, income, and regional location.

Using that list, you can market directly to your leads; develop an ongoing direct mail campaign and/or use their Email addresses to send them ongoing information that may pertain to seniors and aging.

Constructing Your Marketing House

Laying the Foundation

Marketing should be based on a set system so that you can hand it over to someone else to follow the same systems. Think of your marketing systems as a framed building. You need a foundation, which is your logo, tag line, image, and overall branding. From that you need support framing, or "pillars." The pillars hold up your rooftop, which is your sales and business revenue growth. Individually each pillar won't support the whole structure, but as a group they provide the stability and strength to support a roof. The larger your desired organization, the more important numerous pillars and their maintenance becomes.

Marketing Pillars

Building the Support Pillars

The more pillars you create and implement on a regular basis, the more successful your marketing and company growth will be. Integrate as many columns into your marketing plan as possible. You don't have to use every one, however, and you can always add more:

- ❖ Direct Mail

- ❖ Networking

- ❖ Website / Internet

- ❖ Social Media

- ❖ Yellow Pages/Phone Directories

- ❖ Industry Specific Referral Sources

- ❖ Print Ads

- ❖ Directory Listings

- ❖ Newsletters

- ❖ News and Press Releases

- ❖ Sponsored Events

- ❖ Industry Trade Shows

- ❖ Co-Branding efforts

- ❖ Television Advertising

- ❖ Radio Advertising

- ❖ Charitable Activities

- ❖ Public Speaking

Each pillar will take time and effort to create and build. As you create each pillar, build systems around it so it's repeatable.

Direct Mail

Businesses everywhere use direct mail. You see it in your mail every day, and while you may throw out much of it without even opening it, you continue to see a lot of it—because it works.

Direct mail is usually crafted to sell something and has a call to action—i.e., it uses an offer to get you to respond as soon as possible. Your offer should be designed to motivate the reader to take action (e.g., place an order, request more information).

Possible offers could be:

- ❖ A free home safety inspection.

- ❖ A subscription to your newsletter.

- ❖ Information about issues affecting seniors.

- ❖ Buy four hours of home care, get four hours free.

- ❖ 35 percent off first 10 hours of home care.

- ❖ Every 15th visit in a month is free.

- ❖ A seminar on fall prevention, Alzheimer's, or another topic that affects seniors.

- ❖ A free gift for responding to a survey (which is also a qualifying tool of whether someone may need your services).

- ❖ Any service or product that you believe a great number of your clients may be interested in.

Be creative. Choose an offer that carries significant value to prospective clients yet is low cost for you.

There are generally two different types of mailers: a letter or a post card.

Well-written letters, when opened, can present your services in a detailed manner. Key words: when opened. The recipient usually takes only one or two seconds to look at it before deciding whether to open it. The envelope needs to entice the recipient to open it, typically by offering a free gift inside or other irresistible offer. The envelope's appearance, size, and message should be distinct from other mail.

The letter gives you the opportunity to address the recipient's interests or needs. Your letter should start with an outstanding headline. The letter should support the headline using testimonials and stories and further detail the benefits of your offer. The more personal the letter, the more effective the results. Close the letter with the call to action—which is to contact you for the offer. You can provide a contact phone number or include a separate reply card to be mailed back to you.

Postcards, another form of direct mail, are the most read, least expensive form of direct mail marketing. Postcard campaigns are significantly less expensive to print and mail. Postcards are more successful when mailed consistently over a period of time.

Whichever mailing medium you choose, commit to a complete campaign over many months or a year. A response ratio of about 1 percent is very successful. Anything better than that is phenomenal. So if you're hoping to get a response from 40 people, plan to mail out to 4,000.

Direct Mail Books

Learn more on direct mail marketing:

Successful Direct Marketing Methods
By Bob Stone and Ron Jacobs

The Complete Guide to Direct Marketing: Creating Breakthrough Programs That Really Work
By Chet Meisner

Test the results of different approaches; in your next mailing use the response information to improve the responses. For example, do a postcard mailing with two different postcards, each with different message, layout, etc. Determine which one garners a better response, and next time improve on that one—again, with two different variations, always improving on the better response. Eventually you'll have developed a mailing campaign that is proven effective.

Networking

Networking is by far the most cost effective form of marketing. One of the easiest ways of putting yourself in situations to meet people is to join local organizations and industry specific organizations.

* Chamber of Commerce

* Knowledge Networks — i.e,, Health Care Related Organizations that are focused on helping to educate other health care professionals

* Leads Clubs like LeTip or BNI (Business Networking International)

* Community Service Organizations:

    o Rotary

    o Kiwanis

    o Lions Club

    o Soroptomist Club

    o Men's Groups

    o Women's Groups

    o Knights of Columbus

    o Elks Club

    o Jaycees

If you join only one organization, join your local chamber of commerce. The very purpose of community chambers is to promote businesses in the community by sponsoring events and access to helping your business grow and thrive. Chamber organizations, which are in almost every community, provide you immediate access to active members of the business community. Most chambers have monthly networking events that you should plan to attend. And by joining, you'll be listed in the business directory and be provided information and opportunities to market to your community.

Before you attend any networking event, remind yourself that you're there for a purpose: to meet new people and tell others about your business. Set a goal. Place 10 business cards in your right pocket, and make a goal of meeting 10 new people. As you meet each of them, give them one of your cards and get one of theirs in return. Put their cards in your left pocket. You'll know you've reached your goal when your right pocket is empty and your left pocket contains 10 new business cards.

As you meet new business leaders, keep in mind that you're there for the same reason they are: to meet others. They are there to tell you about their business as much as you're there to introduce your business to them. Be prepared with your 30-second commercial and 3-minute commercial about your business. Take a genuine interest in their business. Ask questions about it. The more interest you show, the more memorable an impression you'll leave with them. Given enough time, they'll naturally ask you about what you do.

So, get out and meet new people! If you're introverted or think that you're not good at meeting new people, push yourself out of your comfort zone. Meeting people doesn't require lots of money, but not doing it can cost a great deal by way of missed opportunities.

Website

Having a website for your business is imperative. The website is a medium that can be used in educating your community and clients, recruiting efforts, training efforts, and so much more. Developing one is not difficult—plenty of websites specialize in easy-to-build, inexpensive websites.

Many websites are integrated into business systems. Setting up an online application form will reduce your costs of mailing applications to applicants. You can provide a PDF version so that applicants can download the application, fill it out, and submit it to you. Or you can create an online application that can be submitted directly to you via your website. This not only gives you the application instantly but streamlines your background checks and hiring process.

Your website can be also be integrated to your marketing efforts, and providing relevant articles on your website not only educates readers but helps you become an expert in your field. Include your web address in all print material, business cards, brochures, letterheads, envelopes, and anything else that leaves your office.

If your business doesn't have an email address, get one now—it's as important as your website. In fact, once your domain name is registered and the website set up, begin using an email with that domain name. Most web hosting packages include email address as part of the hosting. It looks more professional, and it promotes your website. If you're using an email address that doesn't have your domain name, begin forwarding all your email to the domain email.

GET YOUR WEBSITE UP TODAY!

Consider the following websites to get your web presence up quickly:

Go Daddy
www.GoDaddy.com

Network Solutions
www.networksolutions.com

Yahoo
http://smallbusiness.yahoo.com

Square Space
www.squarespace.com

Social Media

In the past two years, social media sites such as Facebook, Twitter, Linked In, etc. have become household words. Utilize these sites (which are free) in your marketing efforts.

Social media have provided quality leads to hundreds of thousands of businesses very inexpensively. Many potential clients' decision makers are their children who turn to the web to find solutions for their parents. Integrating the social media into your marketing is essentially creating long-distance relationships with them, often before you've even spoken to them.

Social media offer many marketing opportunities. For example, creating a blog and writing regularly about topics specifically related to seniors can drive targeted prospects to your website, increasing awareness of your company and promoting you as the expert in senior care of your community.

Phone and Directory Listings

Although the Internet has largely negated the need to be in the Yellow Pages, it's still helpful to be listed there. Your telephone number (if it's a land line) is often automatically listed under the name that the phone number is registered as. There are now many different brands of Yellow Pages, and the challenge becomes which one(s) to place ads in. Your competition may have ads in each of them, so research which one is used most within the communities you serve, and determine how much investment it may be worth for each. If you decide not to place an ad in each directory, it's a good idea to still contact each and make sure they will still publish your listing (which is usually free) without an ad.

Many senior-specific directories are published to help seniors navigate the labyrinth of products and services available to them. When you're at the local senior center introducing your business to them, look for these publications. Ask which ones their visitors read the most, and take an issue with you. (Also ask if you can leave some of your brochures at the center.) Some will be non-profit; others are for profit. Call the publications, and ask them what's needed to get listed and what the cost is.

Referral Sources

Referral sources are one of the least expensive and most effective form of getting leads; they involve mostly your time and meeting people. It takes only a few key referral sources to provide you with a number of clients before your business is thriving.

Referral sources are about developing relationships with key people who will refer your company to others that may need your services. They're people in the community who have regular and direct contact with seniors through their work.

These people are found at places such as the following:

- ❑ Adult Day Care Centers
- ❑ Assisted Living Facilities
- ❑ Banking Trust Organizations
- ❑ Churches and Religious Organizations
- ❑ Concert and Arts Associations
- ❑ DME Providers (Durable Medical Equipment)
- ❑ Elder Care Physicians (Geriatric Care)
- ❑ Elder Law Attorneys/Probate Attorneys
- ❑ Funeral Homes
- ❑ Government Agencies with Senior Focus
- ❑ Health Care Professional Networking Groups
- ❑ Home Health Companies
- ❑ Breakfast and Lunch Diners
- ❑ Hospice Service Providers
- ❑ Hospital Discharge Planners
- ❑ Independent Living Communities
- ❑ Long Term Insurance Agents
- ❑ Non-profit agencies
- ❑ Nursing Homes
- ❑ Prescription Drug Pharmacies
- ❑ Retirement and Financial Planners
- ❑ Retirement Homes and Communities
- ❑ Senior Centers

☐ Senior Group Travel Agencies

☐ Social Service Organizations and Agencies

☐ War Veterans Organizations

The above list should help toggle your mind. Brainstorm all the areas in your community that may come into contact with your ideal clients.

Next, contact each of them. Ask when you can drop off some information about your services. Get a face-to-face appointment with them. When you meet them, using your 3 to 5 minute "commercial," explain what you do, how you may benefit some of the seniors they come into contact with. Then ask if they will refer people to you.

Give your new referral sources a reason that they would want to refer clients to you. For example, let them know that any client they refer would be issued 15 percent off or receive four hours free following the first four hours they use your service. Create a coupon for the referral sources to give to the clients they refer to you. Leave behind plenty of business cards and brochures.

Print Ads

Strategically placed print ads, though expensive, can win you quality leads. The key is how effective they are in reaching your target audience to respond.

Newspapers are an obvious choice. Seniors still read newspapers diligently; however, newspaper subscribership is decreasing. Focus on printed papers targeting seniors. Watch for these as you visit senior centers. You can also find them just inside grocery store doors, senior centers, pharmacies, care facilities, and other areas that seniors frequent.

Call the different publications to inquire about their advertising rates. But even if you decide to place an ad, don't sign a long-term contract; they may not be effective in bringing you clients. (You'll know whether they are effective when you ask, "How did you hear about us?")

Keep the following in mind when you place an ad:

- ❖ What your company does should be clearly defined.

- ❖ The benefits your service provides should be clear.

- ❖ Your contact information should be clear and easy to find.

- ❖ The ad should not be cluttered.

- ❖ Seniors can't read small print easily.

- ❖ Don't explain everything in an ad— just enough to grab attention, communicate what you do, and convey how to contact you for more information.

If your ad isn't getting results, consider changing the ad's layout and other visual properties. And if it still isn't performing, pull the ad. Spend your advertising money where it will be most effective.

The following page displays an example of a simple, easy to read print ad.

STAY IN YOUR OWN HOME, LONGER

Stay independent in your own home for as long as possible!
We assist you with daily activities like:

* Meal Preparation
* Light Housekeeping
* Companionship
* Transportation
* Personal Hygiene
* Caregiver Respite

(555) 555-5555
www.yourcompany.com

Insured | Bonded | Screened

Newsletters

Newsletters are an effective way to keep in touch with existing clients and prospective clients relatively inexpensively. Clients appreciate the information and education that newsletters offer. A newsletter is an unobtrusive manner to keep your name in the prospects' mind by providing valuable information to them free of charge. You can also generate new leads through your website by offering a free subscription to your newsletter.

Each issue should present new and valuable information in such a way that clients look forward to receiving it regularly. The newsletter should be formatted in a professional and consistent manner. Articles about senior related topics such as nutrition, active living, changes in prescription Medicare laws, etc. all create value to the recipients.

A monthly or quarterly newsletter requires time and effort to create. Outsourcing the newsletter can save you money and time and result in a higher quality product than you would produce yourself. Every month, a complete and comprehensive, distributable newsletter full of valuable senior related information can be sent to you through www.homecarehowto.com. Add your logo and contact information, and it's ready to print or email in minutes.

News and Press Releases

There are two ways to get your name in newspapers: Pay for advertising or be covered in a news story.

A press release highlights your company's achievements as a news story and prints them as news. Being presented as news carries far more credibility, makes a lasting impression, and is more cost effective than paid advertising. The credibility, impressions, and exposure can bring a significant volume of phone calls and clients—a terrific strategy to jump start your business.

The traditional local newspaper, while a seemingly dying medium, is still read by a large majority of seniors—who also seem to read it cover to cover. But press releases aren't limited to the newspaper; regional publications and the Internet also publish them.

Regional magazines and publications are growing media. From senior specific papers to regional lifestyle and business magazines, these alternative sources of news and information are targeting seniors and their children—in other words, your target audience.

The Internet is forcing newspapers to evolve or dissolve; your clients' offspring increasingly get their news online, don't overlook this medium. Besides, press releases via online news carriers do more than just publish your company's story; they also increase your website's exposure and index-ability for search engines. In turn the children who live far from their parents can find you more easily when they do a web search.

The guidelines for writing a press release that gets printed are different from those for writing advertisements. A well written press release focuses on a story that isn't about the company; instead it's about a newsworthy event or experience that puts your business in a positive light— e.g., the donation of your services or time to a nonprofit organization or coverage of an elderly person whose life was enhanced by your services.

Get Your Press Release Published

Write a press release, and get it published from Press Release Pros:

24-7 Press Release
http://www.24-7pressrelease.com/press_writing_tips.php

Free Press Release
http://www.free-press-release.com

PR Leap
http://www.prleap.com

PR Log
http://www.prlog.org

PR Web
http://service.prweb.com

Writing press releases is as much of an art as a science' entire books are written on the subject. Outsource them to a specialist or learn how to do write them properly yourself, keeping the following points in mind:

* Newspapers and other print publications may focus on different   areas each day, week, or month. Ask the editor what kinds of stories they'll need, and then create releases along the editor's specifications.

* Keep your news releases succinct—100 words is ideal.

* Attach low resolution photographs (72 dpi) to the email.

* Be professional and respectful of an editor's time. Editors are often very busy and have many deadlines.

* Don't disguise an advertisement as a press release. Editors will see right through this.

* Create a Press Kit and have it available on your website for the editor to download.

* Include:

    o The news press release announcing the event or service.

    o A background giving more complete details.

    o A biography of you (the owner/principal) and anyone else mentioned in the release and a history of the company.

    o High resolution photographs of you and anyone mentioned in the release.

* Email your news release to the editor. Include a link to your Press Kit.

* Contact the editor once you've submitted the release. Call him or her and politely request that he or she read it.

Sponsored Events

Sponsoring events that are targeted to seniors and their lifestyles can provide many opportunities to expand increase the company's visibility, image, credibility, and prestige. Consider sponsoring events such as the annual Memory Walk for Alzheimer's Association, local prescription drug disposal programs, and community educational awareness fairs.

Sponsoring events entails providing labor or financial or other resources to support an activity to help reach various business goals. Event sponsorship can complement your other advertising and marketing efforts.

Many of these events get media coverage. By joining the event, you get the opportunity for media coverage that goes far beyond what your own media campaign could accomplish. You also gain credibility. Seniors perceive sponsoring events as supporting the community and being a good business citizen, which creates tremendous goodwill.

Co-Branding

Co-branding is forming marketing synergy by partnering with another company that is complimentary to the senior home care services . You will save on advertising costs and gain access to their client lists. Your partner's clients could potentially become your clients and vice-versa. Complementary companies could include durable medical equipment providers (e.g., DME suppliers), elder law firms, hospice providers, local prescription drug suppliers, or nursing homes.

Co-branding can be used with one or several of the previously marketing strategies. For example, your newsletter could include information from an elder law firm on topics of trusts, wills, and probate. Dual promotion between your website and your co-branding partner is also helpful. Consider sponsoring an event together, or create an event with your partner from the start.

Public Speaking

How do the words public speaking affect you?. Do you cringe and envision yourself tongue-tied in front of a crowd? Many people do. But it's not difficult to overcome the fear of speaking in public; you can do so in a short amount of time. Public speaking is an inexpensive marketing tool that you can use to quickly increase your client base.

Speaking provides tremendous credibility and visibility that increases over time. People notice and remember you and your business when you're in front of a room. The more people that hear you speak and see your business name, the more successful people believe you are. And when you speak to dozens or even hundreds of people at an event, you have their attention all at once while proving yourself as the local expert in your community—and filling your pipeline of potential prospects.

You don't have to be perfect to do an effective job. You need only be adequate to make a good impression. The key is to begin speaking. There are plenty of opportunities for you to speak for free.

Select a topic that will benefit and target seniors, and then give it a catchy title—i.e., "The 10 Signs of Alzheimer's Disease" or "Aging Gracefully—It's About What You Eat."

Find a target audience that will give you a free podium. Many organizations are looking for speakers to give free presentations and educate the community on a variety of topics.

- ❖ Your local senior center

- ❖ Non-profit organizations

- ❖ Community service organizations such as Kiwanis, Rotary, and Lion's clubs

- ❖ Churches

- ❖ Chamber of commerce

- ❖ Professional associations

❖ Health care associations

Still apprehensive? Join a local Toastmasters International group (www.toastmasters.org). Toastmasters' focus is helping people improve public speaking skills and overcoming fears of speaking.

Door Hangers

Door hangers are an inexpensive way to advertise. This method involves only your time and the investment of the printed door hangar cards. The printing services you used for your business cards and brochures can produce door hangars with the same branding.

You (and your family members) can distribute the door hangars, or you can hire it to be done by placing an ad on Craigslist.org or approaching a local boys' and girls' club that is interested in earning money for their clubs. If you do hire someone, make sure you supervise the distribution. Be willing to drive the workers to the areas you want covered and watch them as several go door to door. Otherwise you might get a call from an irritated homeowner who found hundreds of your door hangars in the bushes. Worse, you may not hear anything from anyone because the person you paid to distribute them tossed them into the trash.

Radio Advertising

Radio advertising reaches a mass of targeted audience and at a lower cost than you might think. Targeted properly to either seniors or their children and run enough times, this advertising can drive results to your business quickly.

A successful radio campaign requires numerous factors coming together properly:

❖ Advertising with a radio station that hits your target market.

❖ Running your commercial spot frequently at the right times so it hits your target market the most.

❖ Producing a catchy, memorable commercial spot.

Reaching your target market is essential. Research your area's stations and find the stations that reach the seniors or their children, ages 40-60.

Timing is also crucial. If a station is targeting seniors yet begins playing your radio spot after 9:00 PM, you'll probably miss the mass numbers you're seeking because the potential clients are already in bed. Running the spot at 10 AM talk show time (several times in the hour) will probably be more effective. You'll reach prospects' children through a very different station, and since this audience is probably working at 10 AM, you may miss them at that time. This radio station should play your ads during their drive time to or from work. Request a specific demographic breakdown of each station's listeners so you can make the informed decisions. Also request a breakdown of the times your target listens the most. When you've identified that time, run your ad spot often.

Those who hear a catchy commercial spot several times will remember it. The musical backgrounds, voice actors, and sound effects you use will determine your production costs. The radio station may want to produce a catchy, award winning radio commercial. Just make sure that the commercial is truly selling your services and has a call to action for the listeners so that you'll see results through an increase in clients. Finally, remember that the production costs are in addition to the costs of your ad spots.

Chapter 10 Review Task List

Upon completing Chapter 10 you should ....

be well on your way to getting calls from prospective clients and possibly have signed your first client already. You should also have:

- ☐ Created a marketing plan.

- ☐ Set your marketing goals.

- ☐ Created a leads list.

- ☐ Set your marketing budgets in relation to your client acquisition cost or below.

- ☐ Identified which marketing columns to use.

- ☐ Started developing five or more marketing pillars.

- ☐ Created systems for consistent implementation and maintenance of each marketing column.

- ☐ The tools and systems in place for measuring of marketing results.

With all that's been covered over the last ten chapters, your business should be up, running, and stirring with activity. Understandably, there may be an area or two where you have questions, more in depth explanation or guidance.

If you're challenged in one area or another, take a deep breath in knowing here's more help. By now, hopefully you've already visited www.homecarehowto.com. The many free resources available to you are sure to help. If you feel consulting with a business coach would make the difference - that's available, as well as business start-up classes and other services to help you succeed.

Best wishes to your success!

INDEX

R

S

T

U

V

W

BIBLIOGRAPHY

24-7 Press Release.com. (n.d.). Retrieved from 24-7 Press Release: http://www.24-7pressrelease.com/press_writing_tips.php

99 Dollar Logos.com. (n.d.). Retrieved from 99 Dollar Logos: http://www.99dollarlogos.com

August Systems CRM. (n.d.). Retrieved from August Systems Software: http://www.august-systems.com

Business Incubators . (n.d.). Retrieved from National Business Incubator Association NBIA: http://www.nbia.org/

Business Plan Pro Software. (n.d.). Retrieved from Palo Alto Software (available at Amazon.com): http://www.amazon.com/dp/B000WMQYLA?tag=hom0d8-20&camp=14573&creative=327641&linkCode=as1&creativeASIN=B000WMQYLA&adid=1W40VHRGFPP2GPKCA4MS&

Cactus Mailing Leads and Direct Mail. (n.d.). Retrieved from Cactus Mailing Company: http://www.cactusmailing.com

Craigslist Classified Listings. (n.d.). Retrieved from Craigslist.com: http://www.craigslist.com

Decotiis, T. (Feb, 2008). *Make It Glow: How to Build a Company Reputation for Human Goodness, Flawless Execution, and Being Best-in-Class* (1st ed.). Greenleaf Book Group Press; 1st edition.

Election by a Small Business Company. (n.d.). Retrieved from US Internal Revenue Service: http://www.irs.gov/pub/irs-pdf/f2553.pdf

eRSP Software. (n.d.). Retrieved from Kaleida Systems Software: http://www.ersp.biz

Free Press Release.com. (n.d.). Retrieved from Free Press Release: http://www.free-press-release.com

Generations Home Care Software. (n.d.). Retrieved from Integrated Database Systems (IDBS) : http://www.idb-sys.com

Gerber, M. E. (1995, 2001). *The E Myth Revisited* (2 ed.). New York, NY, USA: Harper Business.

GoDaddy.com. (n.d.). Retrieved from GoDaddy, Inc: http://www.godaddy.com

Google Documents. (n.d.). Retrieved from Google Docs: http://docs.google.com

Hill, N. *Success Through A Positive Mental Attitude.* Pocket .

Hill, N. (1937). *Think and Grow Rich* (12 ed.). CreateSpace.

Incorporate.com . (n.d.). Retrieved from Incorporate.com - The Company Corporation Incorporation Services: http://www.incorporate.com

Info USA.com. (n.d.). Retrieved from Info USA Sales Leads: http://www.infousa.com

IRS - C Corporations . (n.d.). Retrieved from US Internal Revenue Service : http://www.irs.gov/businesses/small/article/0,,id=98240,00.html

IRS - How to Obtain An EIN Number. (n.d.). Retrieved from US Internal Revenue Service (IRS) : http://www.irs.gov/businesses/small/article/0,,id=102767,00.html

IRS - LLC Entities. (n.d.). Retrieved from US Internal Revenue Service (IRS) : http://www.irs.gov/businesses/small/article/0,,id=98277,00.html

IRS - Partnerships. (n.d.). Retrieved from US Internal Revenue Service (IRS) : http://www.irs.gov/businesses/small/article/0,,id=98202,00.html

IRS - S Corporations. (n.d.). Retrieved from US Internal Revenue Service (IRS) : http://www.irs.gov/businesses/small/article/0,,id=98263,00.html

IRS - Sole Proprietorships. (n.d.). Retrieved from US Internal Revenue Service (IRS) : http://www.irs.gov/businesses/small/article/0,,id=98202,00.html

Jacobs, B. S. (2007). *Successful Direct Marketing Methods* (8 ed.). McGraw-Hill.

Kaleida Systems eRSP Home Care Software Solutions. (n.d.). Retrieved from eRSP CRM: http://www.ersp.biz

KanTime Homecare Solutions Software. (n.d.). Retrieved from Kanrad Technologies Inc.: http://www.kantime.com

KIJIJI Classified Listings By Google. (n.d.). Retrieved from KIJIJI.COM: http://www.kijiji.com

Legal Zoom.com. (n.d.). Retrieved from Incorporation Services: http://www.legalzoom.com

List of Leads.com. (n.d.). Retrieved from List of Leads: http://www.listofleads.com

Logo Designs. (n.d.). Retrieved from Logo Design Guru: http://www.logodesignguru.com

Mailing List Shop. (n.d.). Retrieved from Mailing Lists Online Pty Ltd: http://www.mailinglistshop.com/

Mandino, O. (July 2009). *The Greatest Secret*. Bantam.

Meisner, C. (2006). *The Complete Guide to Direct Marketing: Creating Breakthrough Programs That Really Work*. Kaplan Business.

MNC Incorporating Services. (n.d.). Retrieved from My New Company: www.mynewcompany.com

My Corporation. (n.d.). Retrieved from My Corporation Incorporation Services: http://www.mycorporation.com

Network Solutions. (n.d.). Retrieved from Network Solutions Domain Name Whois: http://www.networksolutions.com

Noe, R. (October 23, 2009). *Employee Training and Development*. McGraw-Hill/Irwin.

Peachtree Accounting Software . (n.d.). Retrieved from Sage Software: http://www.peachtree.com

Penny Saver. (n.d.). Retrieved from Penny Saver Publishing: http://www.pennysaverusa.com

Podmoroff, D. (June 2004). *How to Hire, Train & Keep the Best Employees for Your Small Business*. Atlantic Publishing Group Inc.

PR Leap. (n.d.). Retrieved from PR Leap.com: http://www.prleap.con

PR Log. (n.d.). Retrieved from PR Log.com: http://www.prlog.com

PR Web.com. (n.d.). Retrieved from PR Web Services: http://service.prweb.com

Quickbooks Software. (n.d.). Retrieved from Intuit's Quickbooks Software (Available at Amazon.com): http://www.amazon.com/dp/B003YJ5ESM?tag=hom0d8-20&camp=14573&creative=327641&linkCode=as1&creativeASIN=B003YJ5ESM&adid=1X5NA4HYJ4WEBSE2CJNN&

Sage ACT! . (n.d.). Retrieved from ACT! Contact Management Software: http://www.act.com

Sales Contact Leads. (n.d.). Retrieved from Go Leads : http://www.goleads.com

Sales Force CRM Software. (n.d.). Retrieved from Sales Force CRM: http://www.salesforce.com/CRM

Sharp Dots.com. (n.d.). Retrieved from Sharp Dots Printing Services: http://www.sharpdots.com

Square Space Web Sites. (n.d.). Retrieved from Square Space, Inc.: http://www.squarespace.com

Third Age. (n.d.). Retrieved from A Boomer's Guide to a Life of Health, Happiness, Passion, and Purpose: http://www.thirdage.com/today/caregiving/elder-care-startling-statistics#ixzz0qO9DD2Iq

Toastmasters International. (n.d.). Retrieved from Toastmasters International Organization: http://www.toastmasters.org

Tracy, B. *The Ultimate Goals Program: How to Get Everything You Want*. Nightingale-Conant.

Trademarks Review. (n.d.). Retrieved from US Patent Trade Office (USPTO): http://www.uspto.gov/trademarks/index.jsp

UPrinting. (n.d.). *U Printing.com*. Retrieved from U Printing Services: http://www.uprinting.com

US Census Bureau. (n.d.). Retrieved from US Census Bureau: http://www.census.gov/

Vista Print.com. (n.d.). Retrieved from Vista Print Services: http://www.vistaprint.com

Waitley, D. (2007). *The New Dynamics Of Goal Setting*. Harper Perennial.

Yahoo Small Business. (n.d.). Retrieved from Yahoo! - Small Business: http://smallbusiness.yahoo.com

Ziglar, Z. *See You At The Top* (25 ed.). Pelican Publishing.

Zoho CRM Software. (n.d.). Retrieved from Zoho Corporation: http://www.zoho.com

CPSIA information can be obtained at www.ICGtesting.com
Printed in the USA
BVOW07s1851140515

400448BV00002B/110/P